BOWLS OF LOVE

PALEO SOUPS FOR THE SEASONS

ISBN: 978-0-9862256-0-4

Library of Congress Control Number (LCCN): 2014919944

Printed in the United States of America

Edited by: A.J. Walkley (ajwalkley.com)

Photography: Erica Gannett (ericagannett.com)

Design: Margot Harrington (pitchdesignunion.com)

∞ This paper meets the requirements of ANSI/NISO Z39.48-1992 (Permanence of Paper)

BOWLS OF LOVE

PALEO SOUPS FOR THE SEASONS

— BY —

ALI RAKOWSKI

INTERSECTION
COACHING

DEDICATION

For Grandma, whose essence is what this cookbook is all about. A woman who loved more than anyone I've ever known, and who showed it through the delicacies she made and served in her kitchen. Grandma taught me how to share love with bursting affection, how to feed myself and others, and how to truly cherish every bite. Her spirit was electric and unmatched, akin to the vibrancy of beets, the strongest color in my kitchen. I remain connected to Grandma still, with her energy living on through my hands and my heart as I practice her crafts of cooking and sharing love with all those that matter most.

GRATITUDE

- -

Similar to any successful meal, this cookbook was a communal experience and wouldn't be complete without every person who contributed to it. I am forever grateful and impacted by the outpouring of love and support from my 49 bowl-givers. Your bowls and the recipes that live in them on the following pages are forever imprinted on my heart.

To my personal "Board of Directors":

Mom: for eating 75 pounds worth of donuts and ice cream when you were pregnant with me because I was hungry. You have lived your life for me, and I hope this book shows you that I live mine for you.

Dad: for convincing me to love myself as much as you do and to share my authentic self with the world.

Mal: for being the best friend, strategic partner, and irreplaceable other half who taught me what loyalty means.

Sarah: for being my one and only math friend, and the most beautifully well-rounded version of a present-day 1950s housewife.

Laura: for the long walks and even longer talks that fueled my confidence and enthusiasm throughout this process.

Ryan: for falling in love with me even after you saw my bunions. Your patience, support, and faith in me have single-handedly motivated me to reach for my dreams. I am still convinced that the ripple effect of love from this book convinced you to propose to me; either way, my life will be complete when I cook bowls of love for you and our future children around the kitchen island in our future home. I couldn't have dreamt of a better partner, and my heart belongs to you.

CONTENTS

01
FALL

29
WINTER

55
SPRING

81
SUMMER

WHY BOWLS?

When I first came up with the idea for *Bowls of Love*, I knew I wanted to involve as many of my favorite people as possible in some way, shape, or form. For me, cooking has always been a labor of love for the most special people in my life; my first cookbook would be nothing less. The creation of dishes and the eating of them are both communal experiences; if you ask me, food is always meant to be shared. I couldn't think of a better way to share my recipes than in the very bowls used to eat the soups I create.

I reached out to my closest friends and family all over the world, asking them to send me a bowl that had special meaning, that spoke to them, jumped out at them, or intrigued them in some way. Over the course of a few months, I was bowled over (pun intended) at the packages that arrived on my doorstep. There were oval-shaped, circular, and square-shaped bowls; bowls in the form of a pig, decorated with elephants, and a bird perched on top; wooden, ceramic, and even bamboo bowls; bowls with waves, with matching spoons, and bowls that double as mugs. And then there were the colors and patterns – from turquoise to white to peach to purple; from paisley to checkers to flowers to cow spots; bowls with chevron stripes, and ones with hearts and diamonds. Each one I opened revealed a little something about the sender, making the bowls as unique as my relationships and history with every single person, not to mention as distinctive as the soups I created for each.

When all of the bowls aren't being used, they are stacked on a set of beautiful shelves hung with love by my fiancé, Ryan, and his father, David. Seen together on the shelves, I am often overcome by their individuality and the memories every one of them evokes As I sampled all of my recipes out of the eclectic bowls, I was reminded that each dish and bowl in my kitchen is a quiet keeper of the memories of past meals, family events, and the evolution of life. Even when the soups are long gone, the bowls retain the memories of the meal, the company, the traditions surrounding both, and the love passed down from generation to generation.

I have personally crafted every soup recipe in this cookbook for the person who gifted me the bowl associated with it. For me, food always tells a story, and a good story always needs food. We are beyond fortunate to be surrounded by food on a daily basis. It is the fuel that keeps us alive, the medicine that heals, the universal bond that connects, and the most simple and nourishing gift you can give to another person.

I hope you enjoy the *Bowls of Love* I've included in this book and will share the soup recipes with your own loved ones for years to come.

WHAT'S PALEO?

The premise for the recipes in this book is the Paleo diet, which is based on the principal of eating only what was available in the pre-agriculture, Paleolithic era. My cooking is inspired by the main principles of the diet, which include eating grass-fed and pasture-raised meats, wild fish, eggs, fruits, vegetables, nuts, seeds, and unprocessed oils; excluding grains, dairy, legumes, soy, refined sugar, and processed food.
Never a fan of diets, I was drawn to Paleo for two main reasons:

1 / Paleo encourages eating real, clean food
    – food that comes from our Earth and is in
    its original form.

2 / Paleo is an anti-inflammatory diet used by
    many people to strengthen the immune
    system and help heal a variety of ailments.

My experiment with Paleo started back in July of 2012. I was feeling rundown emotionally and mentally, and I was in my 25th year of battling unpredictable stomach issues, allergies, and a host of other "ailments of the day". I was a seemingly healthy person, but I had multiple health-related frustrations. I started to focus my diet on eating organic, sustainably sourced proteins (beef, chicken, fish, etc.) coupled with plentiful portions of fruits and vegetables from my local farmers market. I started to notice small changes at first – weight loss and eczema clearing – and in less than one year, my seasonal allergies and stomach concerns that had negatively impacted my life for over two decades were beginning to taper off.

Eighteen months into a strict Paleo diet, I realized that my digestion issues were not completely healed, so I experimented with certain foods in my diet to achieve a perfect balance. I learned that no diet is "one size fits all". Customization is key to success. Your own Paleo journey should help you achieve a holistic sense of physical, mental, and emotional wellness, and the soups that make up this book are a great starting point.

For those following a strict Paleo diet, please note that the ingredients listed in my recipes are up to your discretion. Salt is optional. Organic canned goods are sometimes offered as an option when fresh isn't available, but keep in mind that local and fresh is always better – and true to Paleo. If you are going to purchase any pre-packaged stock or broth, I highly recommend reading the labels and avoiding options with sugar, stabilizers, and preservatives added. Nut milks and flours can and should be easily made in the comfort of your kitchen, but store-bought alternatives exist for those who want them. I encourage you to experiment with the recipes in my book, customize as needed, and reach out to me with any questions.

The index listed on pages 109-110 includes all of the ingredients used in this book categorized by vegetables; fruits; proteins; nuts & seeds; fats & oils; and herbs, spices, & flavorings. I recommend stocking up on staples like coconut oil, olive oil, humanely sourced meats (the freezer is your friend!), and your favorite spices. You can supplement the staples with weekly trips to the farmers market or grocery store to pick up your favorite fruits and veggies.

I myself am not a doctor, scientist, or an expert. I rely on many experienced professionals for information and guidance in this realm. For those new to Paleo and others who follow out of necessity due to gluten sensitivity, lactose intolerance, or other health-related issues, I am happy to direct you to some great sources that have the specifics around the Paleo diet, the science behind it, and a multitude of additional fantastic recipes to try:

Dr. Loren Cordain
The Paleo Diet
http://thepaleodiet.com

Robb Wolf
The Paleo Solution – The Original Human Diet
http://robbwolf.com

Melissa & Dallas Hartwig
It Starts With Food
http://whole9life.com

Nell Stephenson
Paleoista and *The Paleo Diet Cookbook*
http://paleoista.com

Melissa Joulwan
Well Fed and *Well Fed 2*
http://theclothesmakethegirl.com

George Bryant
The Paleo Kitchen
http://civilizedcavemancooking.com

HOW TO MAKE IT HAPPEN

Inspiring others in the kitchen is not as difficult as you may think. The cooking process includes many activities, some of which start long before a trip to the farmers market or grocery store. The following tips will help you strategically create an environment suited for cooking with love.

01 Eat for Color

When I was a child, my mom had me pick a different color of the rainbow for each day of the week on the calendar. I then had to eat one fruit or vegetable that day of the elected color to get varied nutrients into my picky kid diet. Over the years, I learned how the vibrancy and beauty of colors in food enhance the eating experience. Food preparation can be a creative art form, and a colorful plate stimulates the senses, bringing happiness and energy to your meals while encouraging nutritious eating.

02 Get Creative

Creativity is a must when it comes to keeping things interesting in the kitchen. I love purchasing new cookbooks (like this one!) to experiment with or searching the Web for blogs that focus on specific foods I'm interested in making. You can even look for websites catering to your community to source local ingredients, or widen your hunt around the globe to attempt a classic dish from across the pond. Why not recreate one recipe a month from a site you like or a nation you've never been to? Every meal you make can become a work of art just by choosing the right ingredients with varieties of texture, splashes of color, and garnishes to finish them off. Jazz your meals up a notch with fun placemats, unique plates, and stylish napkins — there's no reason to save such pieces for special occasions when you can enjoy them on a weekly or even nightly basis. Each day and meal is important, and styling your table and food with creativity makes the experience special.

03 Plan Your Grocery Store Experience

You can't create a kitchen of love without doing a bit of shopping first. When you head to the grocery store, shop the perimeter where you'll find the freshest ingredients, including all of the vegetables, fruits, meats, and seafood; the only time I venture further inside is for my nuts and nut butters, oils, vinegars, and home-based needs. Consider picking up one new ingredient you haven't cooked with before every week. I've broadened my horizons and created mouth-watering dishes with kohlrabi, rainbow chard, and bok choy, to name a few. Just because you've only eaten something in a restaurant before doesn't mean you can't cook it yourself in your own home!

Invest in the Right Tools

There are certain tools in the kitchen I can't live without when it is time to make soup:

- Start with a large soup pot – the bigger, the better, so you can make enough leftovers to enjoy all week long.

- Stock your kitchen with at least three cutting boards and some great knives with a sharpener so you can prep all of your ingredients.

- Buy a nice collection of wooden spoons so your family can taste-test as you cook.

- Disposable rubber gloves are great when you are in a rush and don't want your hands covered in raw chicken or dyed purple from your beautiful beets.

- The hand-held immersion blender is the single-best tool for making puréed soups. In a minute or less, you can have a huge pot of perfectly blended soup without having to pull out the food processor or blender. If you don't have one, you can purée soups in batches in a food processor or blender... or you can just invest $30 or less in the tool of your dreams!

- Get a crockpot! Many varieties also available at $30 or less, the crockpot can single-handedly improve your quality of life and stress levels when it comes to meal prep. There are a few recipes in the book I created in the crockpot, but the majority of them can be made in a slow cooker if you'd like.

Chop, Chop, and Chop Some More

Every single time I make soup, I seem to notice that there is one key step – chopping! I truly believe that if you can chop a vegetable, you can become a fantastic soup chef. If you don't like to chop, you can throw everything in a food processor, and you will be ready to go in no time. Pull out all of your ingredients, heat some oil in your pot, chop your veggies, and you'll be on your way to delicious soup! If you have the time, chop double (or even triple) the ingredients in the recipes to make bigger batches. The soups stay fresh for days and even months if you freeze them. This will help you proactively plan ahead for healthy meals in the midst of a busy life. The recipes in the book refer to chopping, dicing, and mincing. An easy way to remember the size order is alphabetical: *Chopping > Dicing > Mincing*. Mincing is the smallest (as small as you can get it), and dicing is usually about half the size of a chop.

Take It to the Island

The kitchen island was where all the magic happened in my house. It was a true vacation, escaping the stress of the day to spend time with my mom as she prepared a meal for our family. I sat on the counter stool watching her every move while I ate a snack, finished homework, or told her all about my day. It is here that I learned how to cook and magically have everything ready at the same time. Whether your kitchen has an island or not, treat it as a true retreat; it is here where you will celebrate your creativity, and create nutritious dishes for yourself and your loved ones. Allow your "island" experience to take you to a happy place every day as you take the time to invest in the health of yourself and your family.

Make it a Family Affair

I've always found my meals are enhanced when I have others to share them with. Growing up, the single most important rule in my house was that my family always ate dinner together, no matter what. There were times when it wasn't easy, but my mom insisted that this was a top priority, so we made it work. We would use the time to catch up on each other's lives, sharing stories and jokes, truly enjoying family time together. Our table created a sense of community, and our friends and neighbors would often ask to join us, making the experience all the more welcoming, loving, and enduring. As I got older, there were multiple phases in my life where I lived alone, and wasn't lucky enough to be surrounded by family and friends. When this happens (as it does at some point for everyone), it is important to still take the time to create a beautiful meal, sit down at the table, and enjoy the hard work that was put into making it.

Focus on Food

If there is one rule to live by around the table, it's to avoid distractions so you are not only fully present to enjoy your meal, but the company of the ones you are eating with as well. Growing up, no phone calls were allowed at dinnertime; our home phone could ring 27 times during dinner, and often did, but no one was allowed to pick up – meal time was family time. This rule now includes cell phones, computers, and the television; none of the aforementioned are allowed once the food reaches the table. There is a lot to appreciate, from the way each ingredient in your dish was grown, to how it got to your home to become prepared into a meal. Take the time to savor each bite, focusing on your body's needs as well as the taste, stepping away from the stress of the day to fully appreciate what you're eating. As a single eater, you should still focus on your food, setting aside all of your devices, and using mealtime as an opportunity for self-reflection, relaxation, and experiencing gratitude.

09 Keep it Simple

When you get down to it, cooking truly can be easy if you let it be. Get organized with a shopping list of ingredients to ensure you have what you need. Prepare your ingredients and follow a recipe, but ultimately follow your instincts! Trust yourself and your taste buds, tasting your food as you cook it. There is no right or wrong answer when it comes to cooking soup – my recipes are simply a guide to fuel your creativity in the kitchen. Depending on your tastes and preferences, feel free to adjust proportions, spices, herbs, and the ingredients themselves. You can even experiment using water as a base instead of stock – I have found that with incredibly farm-fresh ingredients, using water highlights the flavors and allows for a pure, untainted taste.
Like most things in life, practice makes perfect; in cooking, practice tastes perfect.

10 Commit to Your Health

At its essence, food exists to fuel our bodies, and keep us healthy and nourished. I have found that the ultimate remedy for most of my ailments in life can be tracked back to food. Everything from IBS and eczema, to sleep issues and seasonal allergies have been healed or significantly improved through a consistently healthy diet. By making a commitment to your health, you are making a promise to be proactive and stay one step ahead with your meal planning. Eating healthy isn't always the most convenient and easy option, but it is well worth it. Fresh, healthy food is not always available on-the-go, so you'll need to pack snacks and meals ahead of time to ensure you can fuel your body with the good food it deserves. Planning your meals in advance and cooking big batches can make this process easier; invest in some great single-serve storage containers so your meals are pre-portioned and ready for grab-and-go at a moment's notice.

FALL

PIPING PARSNIP & PEAR
FOR CATHERINE RAKOWSKI

My brother, Evan, met his talented wife, Catherine, through Yelp. Two of the biggest foodies out of everyone I know, they were tasting and reviewing their way through New York City when they were both chosen to be Yelp "elites" due to their creative writing talents, humor, and dedication to reviewing all of the hot spots in the city. Thanks to members-only events, Evan met Catherine and the rest is history. He fell in love with her intelligence, beauty, sense of humor, and incredible set of talents; aside from professional singing and acting, Catherine is a pro in the kitchen. In fact, their first dinner party together was a joint meat party for which Evan cooked my mom's famous family rib recipe and Catherine made North Carolina-style BBQ. I wanted my brother to find a wife with many skills, but cooking had to be one, and Catherine does not disappoint. I am so grateful he has found someone so full of love (and recipes) to share his life with.

Catherine's bowl is a fan favorite and was featured in my Kickstarter campaign. The bird perched on the edge of the bowl perfectly embodies Catherine's singing, especially when she's cooking in the kitchen. Handmade from Clay By Jamie's Etsy shop, it is absolutely gorgeous and the perfect vessel to hold our first autumn soup.

INGREDIENTS:

Serves: 4-5

Prep time:
20 minutes

Cook time:
75 minutes

Tip:
The number of portions provided for all of the soups is simply a guide. The actual portions will greatly depend on the size of your bowls, who is eating, how hungry they are, and if the soup is a main course or side dish.

1 Tbsp. olive oil

1 large sweet onion, chopped

3 cloves garlic, chopped

2 pears, peeled & chopped

2 stalks celery, chopped

2 large parsnips (1 ½ lb.), peeled & chopped

3 cups organic chicken or vegetable stock

1 tsp. olive oil

½ cup raw, organic pumpkin seeds

½ tsp. cinnamon

½ tsp. paprika

½ tsp. cumin

Salt & pepper to taste

INSTRUCTIONS:

1 / Heat 1 Tbsp. olive oil over medium heat.

2 / Add onion and garlic, and sauté about 10 minutes until fragrant.

3 / Add pears, celery, and parsnips. Stir well to combine and cook another 5 minutes.

4 / Add stock and bring to a boil.

5 / Cover and reduce heat. Cook for 1 hour.

6 / Meanwhile, heat 1 tsp. olive oil in a small pan over medium heat.

7 / Add pumpkin seeds and toss to combine.

8 / After 1-2 minutes, add cinnamon, paprika, and cumin.

9 / Cook for another 2-3 minutes until fragrant, and then let cool.

10 / When soup is done, let cool slightly and blend with immersion blender or food processor.

11 / Season with salt and pepper to taste. Serve piping hot with 1 Tbsp. of spiced pumpkin seeds on top.

THANKSGIVING IBBIES
FOR GARY TOPCHE

When I think of my Uncle Gary, there are three absolutes that come to mind: he is the best accountant I've ever had, he is an expert fisherman, and he can remember the details of every meal he has ever eaten. Literally. Eating good food with Uncle Gary is an experience I look forward to every year, especially at Thanksgiving. As soon as our turkeys are ready – both lovingly named Tom, year after year – Uncle Gary pulls me into the kitchen to serve as his carving assistant so I can taste a "few" pieces of juicy dark meat while he expertly carves the Toms. Most years this job has been easy, except for the few times when I had to avoid paying attention to his apron, sporting a surprisingly realistic image of Michelangelo's The David. The turkey at the table with the rest of the family, while still delicious, could never compare to the hand-picked bites straight from Uncle G.

After these big holiday feasts, we always have leftovers. A typical family meal for 20 involves cooking for 40, and the morning after consists of divvying up the leftovers to take home. In Yiddish, the leftovers are called "ibbergerblibbernis" – to no surprise, none of us could ever pronounce this word as kids (or adults!). Ibbies for short became the go-to phrase, and the following recipe is the perfect soup to make with your Thanksgiving ibbies.

INGREDIENTS:

INSTRUCTIONS:

Serves: 4

Prep time:
10 minutes

Cook time:
30 minutes

1 Tbsp. olive oil

1 medium onion, chopped

3 stalks celery, chopped

2 cloves garlic, minced

2 small sweet potatoes, chopped

1 tsp. dried sage

¼ tsp. dried thyme

¼ tsp. dried rosemary

¼ tsp. dried marjoram

6 cups turkey or chicken stock

½ cup unsweetened, dried cranberries

1 lb. cooked turkey, shredded

½ tsp. salt

¼ tsp. pepper

Fresh sage leaves (optional)

1 / **Heat oil over medium heat.**

2 / **Sauté onion, celery, and garlic for 10 minutes.**

3 / **Add sweet potatoes and herbs, and cook for another 10 minutes, stirring frequently.**

4 / **Add stock, cranberries, turkey, salt, and pepper, and bring to a boil.**

5 / **Simmer uncovered over medium heat for 10 minutes or until sweet potatoes are soft.**

6 / **Optional: Serve topped with flash-fried sage and a sprinkle of coarse sea salt.**

BROOKLYN BEETS
WITH ROASTED CASHEW CREAM
FOR CESIA RAKOWSKI

Visits to Grandma's always began in the most beautifully predictable way. As we approached the Flatbush neighborhood, the excitement would build, and as we turned the corner onto East 56th Street, there she was – standing on the terrace, elated beyond belief, with enthusiasm oozing out of her in every direction. After Mom or Dad parked, we would run upstairs to her second-floor walk-up for a flood of hugs, kisses, and an immediate snack or two (it had been at least an hour since our last meal!). From the moment we stepped inside, we were surrounded by a special type of love that is a lost art form. Grandma was a survivor in every sense of the word, and she literally lived to love. She shared that love in special "Grandma" cookies, apple crumb cake that over the years became more crumbs than cake, and the best bagels and lox in town. In the midst of all of the meals and snacks, there was always a little bowl of raw cashews on the corner of her white Formica countertop. As I watched her move about the kitchen and listened to her stories in her perfect Polish accent, I would snack on the creamy nuts and dream of the future when I would create and inspire a family in this way. To this day, every time I eat a cashew, I close my eyes for a brief second and get transported right back to Brooklyn with Grandma by my side, my heart and soul surrounded by her love.

Serves: 4-5

Prep time:
20 minutes +
1 hour to soak
cashews

Cook time:
60 minutes

Tip:
You can make your own cashew milk by soaking 1 cup of raw cashews in filtered water for at least 4 hours (I usually do it overnight). Drain and rinse the cashews thoroughly and then add them to a blender with 2 cups of water. Blend slowly at first and then on high once the nuts break down. Add an additional 1-2 cups water based on your preference for the thickness of the nut milk. You can store the milk in an airtight container in the refrigerator for 3-4 days.

INGREDIENTS:

Soup:
4 large beets, peeled & quartered

1 Tbsp. coconut oil

Fine sea salt & coarse ground black pepper to taste

4 cups vegetable stock

1 cup cashew milk

3 cloves garlic, roasted

¼ tsp. turmeric

Cashew cream:
⅓ cup cashews, soaked

1 head garlic

1 tsp. olive oil

1 tsp. lemon juice

⅓ cup cashew (or almond) milk

Fine sea salt & coarse ground black pepper to taste

INSTRUCTIONS:

1 / **Soak your cashews in filtered water for at least 45 minutes prior to starting.**

2 / **Preheat oven to 375 degrees.**

3 / **Scrub, peel, and quarter your beets, drizzling them with the coconut oil, and sprinkling sea salt and pepper on top.**

4 / **With your hands (gloves recommended!), massage until they are coated evenly with the coconut oil.**

5 / **Roast for about 45-60 minutes on a foil- or parchment-lined baking sheet, and then let them cool.**

6 / **Meanwhile, to prepare the roasted garlic, peel off any loose, outer layers, and then cut the top ¼-½ inch off the bulb to expose the cloves.**

7 / **Drizzle the garlic with the olive oil, and roast it for 20-25 minutes until soft and lightly browned.**

8 / **When the garlic cools, remove the cloves (reserving 3 for the soup), and combine them with the soaked cashews, lemon juice, cashew milk, and sea salt and pepper to taste in a blender or food processor.**

9 / **Blend the cashew cream until smooth and then set aside.**

10 / **Combine the roasted beets, stock, cashew milk, 3 garlic cloves, and turmeric.**

11 / **Purée until smooth, and season with salt and pepper to taste.**

12 / **Serve topped with a drizzle of the cashew cream.**

ITALIAN SAUSAGE & BROCCOLI RABE
FOR JOANN BRAUN

When I interviewed for my first job after college as a retirement actuary and met Joann, she took me under her wing and helped me build a solid foundation for my career. Ten years older than me, this fellow outgoing math geek helped me see the person I wanted to become as we grew closer. We used to spend our lunch breaks at Cappriccios or Coldstone in Stamford, CT, chatting about everything from work to our love lives, and everything in between. I cried my eyes out over a Mudpie Mojo, overwhelmed with joy the day Joann told me she was pregnant. I watched her belly grow, asked 1,000 questions, and even investigated her mysterious belly stripe on a weekly basis. While she rightly wanted to disown me after I told her I was going the Paleo route – no more ice cream! – our friendship has remained strong as career changes and geographical moves took us apart. She is the older sister I never had who I will look up to, respect, and love for the rest of my life.

For Joann, I wanted to make an Italian soup to celebrate her ancestry (her maiden name is Voltaggio, after all) and to try out my own skills considering I'm about to marry into an Italian family myself!

INGREDIENTS:

INSTRUCTIONS:

Serves: 4

Prep time:
10 minutes

Cook time:
45 minutes

1 ½ lb. broccoli rabe, cut into 1-inch pieces

1 Tbsp. olive oil

1 ½ lb. chicken sausage (or a sausage of your choosing), casing removed

1 medium onion, chopped

1 Tbsp. garlic, chopped

1 tsp. sea salt

(1) 28 oz. can diced tomatoes

4 cups chicken stock

½ tsp. pepper

1 / Boil a small pot of salted water.

2 / Add broccoli rabe and boil for 4-5 minutes.

3 / Remove broccoli rabe and rinse with cold water to stop the cooking process.

4 / Heat oil over medium heat.

5 / Add chicken sausage and cook for 10-15 minutes, until lightly browned.

6 / Add onion, garlic, and sea salt, and cook for 10 minutes until soft.

7 / Add the tomatoes, stock, and pepper, and bring to a boil.

8 / Cover, reduce heat to medium-low, and cook for 15 minutes.

BRIDE-TO-BE BUTTERNUT SQUASH BISQUE
FOR MARGOT GEORGE

Margot has been a very agreeable guinea pig as I've tried out all of my health coaching and fitness regimens on her. As a client, Margot was such a believer that she'd email me the menus of the restaurants she was going to be eating at so I could choose her meal before she even stepped through the door. We did a two-month workout program that consisted of one rule: no sweating allowed. With only 45 minutes to exercise on our lunch breaks, we didn't have time to shower, or fix our hair or makeup, so the exercises had to be quite calm. If our temperature rose too much, we would take a break, drink water, and fan each other extensively. Margot and I both got engaged just 20 days apart, and now that we are brides-to-be we will begin our special "shedding for the wedding" program. I had to break the news to her that sweating would unfortunately be required this time around.

Our very first cooking date was in the big, beautiful kitchen at Margot's apartment where I taught her how to make my famous butternut squash soup that is just as rich, smooth, and tasty each and every time I make it. Many of my bowl-givers requested to be tied to this recipe, but I had to give it to Margot. The soup came out better than ever the night we made it, even though it took me over 30 minutes to peel the squash!

INGREDIENTS:

INSTRUCTIONS:

Serves: 4

Prep time:
15 minutes

Cook time:
65 minutes

Tip:
Squash and apples can be roasted for 30 minutes at 400 degrees prior to being added to the pot if you have the time and are in the mood for a deeper flavor.

1 Tbsp. coconut oil

2 medium sweet onions, chopped

1 leek (whites only), sliced

1 Tbsp. garlic, chopped

2 ½-3 lb. butternut squash, peeled & cubed

1 apple, peeled & chopped

1 qt. vegetable or chicken stock

2 tsp. cinnamon, divided

1 tsp. salt

½ tsp. pepper

¼ cup raw pecans, chopped

1 / Heat oil over medium heat.

2 / Add onion, leek, and garlic.

3 / Sauté for 5-10 minutes until soft.

4 / Add squash and apple, and cook another 5 minutes.

5 / Add stock and 1 tsp. cinnamon, and bring to a boil.

6 / Cover, reduce heat to low, and simmer for 45 minutes.

7 / Blend soup until smooth, and season with salt and pepper.

8 / Toss pecans with remaining 1 tsp. of cinnamon, and lightly toast or sauté for 4-5 minutes until fragrant.

9 / Serve soup topped with spiced pecans.

PRESIDENTIAL MEXICAN CHICKEN "TORTILLA" SOUP

FOR BRANDON RAKOWSKI

Sometimes I forget that my brother, Brandon, is 12 years younger than me. He has always been an old soul, wise beyond his years. He is the best kitchen companion and taste-tester, trying just about anything I put in front of him, even if he claims to hate it (many of his favorite foods resulted in me forcing him to try them!). While he may not be the best chopper, he keeps me company on the kitchen stool and plays DJ on my computer so the room is filled with great music as he tells me about all of the things going on in his life. Brandon has made me so proud over the years with his many talents in school, theater, and politics. He has a confidence and sense of self that many adults are still striving for, and his impact on the people around him and the world have been and will be great. I certainly plan to vote for Brandon in the 2040 presidential election, assuming he lets me run the White House garden and kitchen.

Brandon's soup is one we made together on a crisp fall day. As we prepared all of the ingredients, Brandon told me that I am going to make a great mom one day. Those simple words meant the world to me, and I will forever think of him when I make this soup.

INGREDIENTS:

Serves: 6

Prep time:
15 minutes

Cook time:
4-8 hours

1 sweet onion, chopped

1 medium shallot, diced

1 red bell pepper, diced

2 lb. chicken breast (fresh or frozen)

2 tsp. cumin

½ tsp. cayenne pepper

1 tsp. garlic powder

1 tsp. salt

½ tsp. pepper

Juice of 2 limes

(1) 4 oz. can green chilies

(1) 28 oz. can fire roasted tomatoes

6 cups chicken stock

Salt & pepper to taste

1 avocado, sliced (optional)

1 large tomato, diced (optional)

Fresh cilantro (optional)

INSTRUCTIONS:

1 / **Arrange chopped onion, shallot, and bell pepper on the bottom of the crockpot.**

2 / **Put raw chicken on top.**

3 / **Add cumin, cayenne pepper, garlic powder, salt, pepper, and lime juice on top of the chicken.**

4 / **Add green chilies, fire roasted tomatoes, and stock.**

5 / **Cook on high for 4 hours or on low for 6-8 hours.**

6 / **Remove the chicken, shred it, and return it to the crockpot.**

7 / **Add salt and pepper to taste.**

8 / **Serve a bowl with sliced avocado and fresh chopped tomatoes on top. You can also add cilantro if you remember... I didn't!**

AUTUMN HARVEST ACORN SQUASH SOUP
FOR LINDA HARTZ

My mom's friend, Linda, immediately wanted to get involved when she heard about *Bowls of Love*. She told me that the concept of the book spoke to her because it mirrored the love that her mom, Jan, created in the kitchen. Jan was born to be a mother and was as unselfish as they come, always prioritizing her family; a large part of that included cooking and having meal time with her husband and children. Though she had no formal training in the kitchen, the food was always delicious, and the effort, pure joy, and love she put into it made every meal memorable. At Christmas, she would bake for days, preparing all of the traditional family treats; and on New Year's Eve, she would make fancy party sandwiches. There were fresh hot donuts on cold winter days and warm chocolate chip cookies for when the kids got home from school. Even at the end of her life when she was suffering terribly with cancer, she gave one last traditional "Jan Christmas Celebration". At the end of the night she was curled up at the end of the couch, so frail and tired, her eyes beaming with love at the sight of her family eating her goodies, and telling their favorite stories of Christmases past.

Jan always loved autumn, especially pumpkins, squash, and freshly ground nutmeg; she always wore muted yellows and oranges, the colors of the season. This soup was designed for Jan and is filled with all of the TLC that she used to create in her kitchen.

INGREDIENTS:

Serves: 4

Prep time:
20 minutes

Cook time:
90 minutes

2 large acorn squash, halved & seeded

Water

2 Tbsp. coconut oil

1 large sweet onion, chopped

2 cloves garlic, diced

4 cups chicken or vegetable stock

½ tsp. ground nutmeg

½ tsp. ground cinnamon

½ tsp. salt

¼ tsp. pepper

Maple syrup and/or nutmeg (optional)

INSTRUCTIONS:

1 / **Preheat oven to 425 degrees.**

2 / **Put the squash in a deep baking dish, cut side down, with water to cover the bottom inch of the dish.**

3 / **Bake for 40-50 minutes until a fork can easily pierce the squash.**

4 / **Remove from the oven, flip squash, and let cool.**

5 / **Heat oil over medium heat.**

6 / **Add onion and garlic, and cook for about 10 minutes until soft and fragrant.**

7 / **Peel the squash flesh out of the skin and add it to the pot.**

8 / **Add the stock, nutmeg, and cinnamon.**

9 / **Bring to a boil and then simmer covered over medium-low heat for 20 minutes.**

10 / **Remove lid, let cool slightly, and purée the soup.**

11 / **Season with salt and pepper – season slowly and taste as you go as some people prefer this soup on the sweeter side.**

12 / **Serve topped with a drizzle of fresh maple syrup and/or some extra freshly ground nutmeg.**

TOM YUM WITH CHICKEN & SHRIMP
FOR LUCI ZIMMERMAN

Eric and his wife, Luci, are my cousins that live the closest to me. I love seeing them and their kids, oftentimes around the dining table sharing a great meal. We celebrated Passover together this year, and we all listened and smiled as their son, Matty, read the Haggadah for the first time. We helped Matty and Mia search for the Afikomen, and they cheered on my fiancé, Ryan, as he tried gefilte fish – an acquired taste, to be sure. We love swapping stories over coffee and dessert about our favorite high schoolers, since Eric hired me as a math tutor for his company, EZ Tutoring. I think Luci's and Eric's love for me exponentially grows each time I bring them a double order of my famous oatmeal raisin cookies – which used to be payment for them driving me to and from family events. I've always claimed that I didn't know my own secret behind those delectables that turned out perfectly soft and gooey on the inside, and crisp on the outside every single time. I use extra handfuls of walnuts and raisins, and press each cookie into the perfect bite-sized treat. Since following a Paleo lifestyle, Luci has taken up the cookie-making torch, which led me to admit that my "secret" was simply following the recipe under the top of the Quaker Oats container... Cookies, however, don't necessarily make for a good soup, so I decided to make a beautiful and flavorful Asian-inspired soup for Luci and her family to enjoy.

INGREDIENTS:

Serves: 6

Prep time:
15 minutes

Cook time:
35 minutes

1 Tbsp. coconut oil

½ jalapeño, diced

2 cloves garlic, chopped

1 red bell pepper, sliced

(2) 14 oz. cans full-fat coconut milk

4 cups vegetable or fish stock

1-inch knob of ginger, peeled & chopped into 4 pieces

1 stalk lemongrass, peeled & cut into 1-inch pieces

1 lb. chicken breast, cut into 1-inch pieces

Juice from 2 limes

1 Tbsp. Thai fish sauce

1 tsp. Thai chili sauce

1 lb. peeled & deveined shrimp, tails removed

1 ½-2 cups mushrooms, sliced

1 cup cherry tomatoes, halved

Salt & pepper to taste

¼ cup fresh cilantro

INSTRUCTIONS:

1 / Heat oil over medium heat.

2 / Add jalapeño, garlic, and bell pepper, and cook for 5 minutes.

3 / Add coconut milk, stock, ginger, and lemongrass, and bring to a boil.

4 / Cover and simmer over medium-low heat for 15 minutes.

5 / Add the chicken, lime juice, fish sauce, and chili sauce.

6 / Bring to a boil again, and then cover and simmer over medium heat for 10 minutes until chicken is cooked through (no pink).

7 / Remove the ginger and lemongrass from the soup, and then add the shrimp, mushrooms, and tomatoes.

8 / Simmer for another 3 minutes until shrimp is cooked through.

9 / Season with salt and pepper to taste, and garnish with fresh cilantro.

CURRIED PUMPKIN & PEAR
FOR RANDI TOPCHE

My mom's younger sister, my Aunt Randi, is without a doubt the fittest granni I know. A mom of three and granni of five, Aunt Randi hits the gym every day and has walked the 40-mile Avon Walk for Breast Cancer in NYC annually for the past 13 years. She inspires me with her dedication and love for her family, and she always comforts me when I miss my mom because they are so similar. Sitting on her kitchen stool and watching her cook, I can close my eyes and convince myself I'm home with my own mother. They have the same sayings, jokes, recipes, and dishes, and they even look alike! Unlimited memories of Thanksgiving and other special occasions come to mind when I think of Aunt Randi. As a vegetarian, her kids tell her that she only eats twigs and berries, but she appreciates all of the colorful vegetable creations I make for the holidays. We salivate together over the tri-color beet salad, and the roasted Brussels sprouts with pomegranate seeds and toasted pecans, while everyone else is busy with the stuffing and mac 'n cheese. Though she doesn't eat any of the meat herself, she makes a killer turkey and once prepared the biggest beef rib roast I've ever seen at almost 20 pounds! Considering all of the holiday memories and traditions that she's instilled in me, I had to make a perfect orange Thanksgiving soup to play up the beautiful turquoise bowl she chose for me.

INGREDIENTS:

Serves: 3-4

Prep time:
10 minutes

Cook time:
30 minutes

Tip:
if you prefer a thicker, creamier pumpkin soup, substitute the stock for two cups water and 2 cups coconut milk.

1 Tbsp. coconut oil

1 medium onion, chopped

2 stalks celery, chopped

1 sweet pear, peeled & chopped

2 tsp. curry powder

2 cups mashed pumpkin, cooked (an organic can of 100% pumpkin is okay in a pinch)

2-3 cups vegetable or chicken stock

½ tsp. salt

⅛ tsp. pepper

Maple syrup (optional)

Chives (optional)

INSTRUCTIONS:

1 / Heat oil over medium heat.

2 / Add onion and celery, and cook for 5-10 minutes.

3 / Add pear and cook another 5 minutes.

4 / Add curry and cook another minute, stirring frequently.

5 / Add the pumpkin and stock, and bring to a boil.

6 / Return heat to low and simmer covered for 15 minutes.

7 / Purée, and season with salt and pepper.

8 / Top with a drop of maple syrup (if you're feeling sweet) and some fresh chives.

NOLA SEAFOOD & SAUSAGE GUMBO
FOR DAVID CARAVELLA

You can't help but look at your fiancé's father and imagine that's what your husband-to-be will be like in 30 years. If that's the case, I am in good shape! David is always working on house projects, the newest being a complete renovation of his 700-square-foot shed at the family lake house in South Salem, NY. Weekend after weekend, David is pouring concrete, constructing walls, installing the electricity, and painting. His signature look is shirtless with ripped jean shorts, work boots, a cigar in hand, and his black dog, Lucy, in his white pickup truck by his side. You would think he was a general contractor, but this is simply a hobby on the side of a wildly successful career in sales. David's generosity and love for his family are unmatched, and he has made me feel like one of his own from day one. He knows how to throw a killer party with his huge Italian family, and you can always rest assured that there will be a great charcuterie platter, the freshest shrimp, and the juiciest meat on the grill. With that fact and his affection for New Orleans (where his daughter went to college) in mind, I have crafted a New Orleans Cajun gumbo with chorizo sausage, chicken, and shrimp. It is the perfect meal for the man on the go, and can be made in the crockpot if you are too busy building and rebuilding to cook!

INGREDIENTS:

Serves: 6

Prep time:
15 minutes

Cook time:
8 hours

1 lb. chicken breast

1 lb. chorizo or Andouille sausage, sliced

1 large onion, chopped

2 stalks celery, chopped

1 green bell pepper, chopped

3 cloves garlic, finely sliced

1 Tbsp. oregano

1 Tbsp. thyme

1 Tbsp. basil

1 Tbsp. paprika

1 tsp. onion powder

1 tsp. garlic powder

¼ tsp. cayenne pepper

1 tsp. salt

½ tsp. pepper

4 cups chicken stock

(1) 28 oz. can diced tomatoes

1 lb. shrimp, peeled & deveined, tails removed

INSTRUCTIONS:

1 / **Combine all ingredients in the crockpot.**

2 / **Cook on low for 7-8 hours.**

3 / **Add shrimp and cook for another 10 minutes.**

4 / **Serve piping hot after a hard day's work.**

Tip:
Try this soup served over cauliflower rice. Pulse one head of cauliflower in a food processor until it looks like rice. Sauté 1 small chopped onion and two cloves of garlic in 1 Tbsp. of olive oil for 5-10 minutes over medium heat until soft. Add cauliflower and cook covered for 10 minutes until cooked through. Season with salt, pepper, herbs of your choosing, and a dash of cayenne pepper!

CREAMY CHESTNUT & ROASTED GARLIC SOUP
FOR ELLE TOPCHE

Elle is my cousin, Brett's, wonderful wife whom I met back in 2006 at our family's Passter (Passover + Easter) celebration at my house. We were having an Easter egg hunt to look for the Afikomen (confusing, I know!) and Elle learned I had a bit of a competitive side. I had broken my finger during a sorority flag football tournament, so I had a cast around my hand and metal pins sticking out of my bone. Injury and all, I pushed everyone out of the way as soon as the search began and collected the eggs like an absolute crazy woman – Elle was legitimately afraid of my intensity, especially when I accomplished the impossible to win the competition. A few years later, my first consulting job sent me to Philadelphia for training near Elle's and Brett's place, and I was given the opportunity to make a much better second impression. We would meet up after work and taste our way through the city, sampling every Steven Starr restaurant one-by-one; from cocktails and dim sum at Buddakan, to margaritas and tableside guacamole at El Vez. For Elle's soup, I wanted to create a dish with the comforts of the fall season since many of our favorite memories take place around the Thanksgiving table. Since she is always trying to get me to drink and be silly, I think the inclusion of sherry wine will surely be appreciated.

INGREDIENTS:

Serves: 4-6

Prep time:
10 minutes

Cook time:
80 minutes

1 head garlic

¼ cup olive oil, divided

2 cups chestnuts, peeled & roasted

2 shallots, chopped

1 onion, chopped

4 stalks celery, chopped

2 cups dry sherry

4 cups vegetable stock or water

Salt & pepper to taste

INSTRUCTIONS:

1 / **Preheat oven to 400 degrees.**

2 / **Peel the excess outside layers of the garlic skin and chop the top ¼- to ½-inch of the garlic head to expose the cloves.**

3 / **Drizzle 1-2 tsp. olive oil over the garlic, wrap in tin foil, and place on a baking sheet.**

4 / **Make ⅛-inch incisions into your chestnut shells until you hit the flesh, and go around almost the full circumference before placing them on the baking sheet.**

5 / **Bake the garlic and chestnuts for 30 minutes.**

6 / **While garlic cools, peel the shells and skin from the hot chestnuts using a towel and discard.**

7 / **Heat 2 Tbsp. olive oil over medium-high heat.**

8 / **Add shallots, onion, and celery, and cook over medium-high heat about 10 minutes until soft.**

9 / **Add chestnuts and roasted garlic, and continue cooking until onions start to caramelize (about 20 minutes).**

10 / **Add sherry to deglaze – add sherry, bring to a boil, and scrape the bottom of the pan with a wooden spoon, releasing the brown bits, and stirring constantly until the liquid reduces by about half (about 5-10 minutes).**

11 / **Add stock and simmer covered over medium-low heat for 10 minutes.**

12 / **Purée until smooth, and then season with salt and pepper to taste.**

13 / **Serve with remaining olive oil.**

TEDDY BEAR BUTTERNUT BEEF CHILI
FOR RICHARDO FRANCIS

Chardo, Chardino, Char-Char – no matter what name he's called at any given time, this man is a true gem. As my brother, Evan's, best friend, fraternity brother, and roommate for many years, my Char-Char teddy bear has become a staple member of our clan. Chardo takes part in all family activities, including our famous Catch Phrase competitions. He somehow manages to be the worst Catch Phrase player on the planet, but the games aren't complete without him. When the timed beeping game console gets into his hands, he looks at his word, laughs, looks at Evan, and stutters. He sometimes manages to get a clue or two out, and to our surprise, Evan always miraculously knows the answer. Chardo's smile and spirit light up every family event, and he even somehow became the best latke maker in our entire family.

For his soup, I wanted to combine the heartiness of beef chili with the sweetness of butternut squash to represent the strong and sweet teddy bear that he is through and through.

INGREDIENTS:

INSTRUCTIONS:

Serves: 6-8

Prep time:
15 minutes

Cook time:
1 hour

2 lb. ground beef

1 tsp. salt

½ tsp. pepper

1 Tbsp. olive oil

1 sweet onion, diced

1 small shallot, diced

4 cloves garlic, minced

1 red bell pepper, chopped

1 ½ Tbsp. chili powder

1 ½ Tbsp. cumin

1 ½ Tbsp. smoked paprika

2 tsp. cinnamon

1 Tbsp. oregano

½ cup tomato paste

8 cups beef stock

3 lb. butternut squash,
peeled & cubed

1 bunch kale, roughly chopped

Salt & pepper to taste

Fresh oregano (optional)

1 / Season ground beef with salt and pepper, and cook in a large stock pot about 7-10 minutes until there is no pink.

2 / Drain the fat from the pot and set the meat aside.

3 / Add oil, onion, shallot, garlic, and bell pepper to the pot.

4 / Cook for 10 minutes or until onions begin to soften.

5 / Add the meat back to the pot along with the spices, herbs, tomato paste, beef stock, and squash.

6 / Bring to a boil, and then simmer covered over medium-low heat for 30 minutes or until squash is soft.

7 / Add kale and cook another 5-10 minutes until wilted.

8 / Add additional salt and pepper to taste, and top with fresh oregano if desired.

SOWA FARMERS MARKET CHICKEN SOUP
FOR CHRIS MARTENS

Chris and I were both living in Boston when we independently signed up for the annual New York City 40-mile walk for breast cancer with the Avon Foundation. Chris had requested a walking buddy and the next thing we knew, we were walking hundreds of miles around Boston and Cambridge together. Chris is a special soul with a deep love for yoga, the Grateful Dead, and kale smoothies (sometimes made from the scraps of the meals I'd made the day before). She opened my eyes to so many things in the world, and taught me about everything from mercury retrograde to "freecycle" – reusing and recycling goods with your community to keep them out of the landfill. She's accompanied me to countless farmers markets around Boston, and she was by my side as I started my Paleo journey, began my blog, and studied to become a health coach. My talks and walks with Chris in Boston single-handedly kept me strong during a very challenging time in my life. My favorite memories were the simplest afternoons where we strolled through the SOWA market after a long walk, tasting the local treats, and trying to find the most inappropriately shaped squashes at the market, making this soup particularly fitting for Chris.

INGREDIENTS:

INSTRUCTIONS:

Serves: 6-8

Prep time:
20 minutes

Cook time:
2 hours

2 Tbsp. olive oil

2 medium sweet onions, chopped

2 shallots, chopped

1 leek (whites and greens), thinly sliced

5 cloves garlic (about 2 Tbsp.), chopped

3 lb. free-range organic chicken

Sea salt, pepper, paprika, & thyme

3 carrots, peeled & chopped

3 parsnips, peeled & chopped

1 bunch flat-leaf parsley

1 bunch dill

8+ cups water or stock

1 bunch kale

1 / Heat oil over medium heat.

2 / Add onion, shallots, leek, and garlic, and cook for 10 minutes until fragrant.

3 / Place the whole chicken on top of the mixture, and season generously on both sides with salt, pepper, paprika, and thyme.

4 / Add carrots, parsnips, parsley, and dill.

5 / Cover the chicken and vegetables with your water or stock (you can use half and half if you'd like).

6 / Bring the pot to a rapid boil, and then simmer covered over medium-low heat for at least 90 minutes (more is fine!).

7 / Take the herbs and chicken out of the pot, remove the skin and bones, and add all shredded meat back into the pot.

8 / Break your kale into 1-inch pieces, add to the pot, and cook for another 5 minutes until wilted.

WINTER

QUINTESSENTIAL WINTER BEEF STEW
FOR LAURA DALEY CARAVELLA

I couldn't dream of a better mother-in-law if I tried. Laura's résumé is a mile-long as my friend, mentor, and surrogate mom. I am eternally grateful to her for raising Ryan, and I am so lucky to have her as a partner for weekly walks, brainstorming sessions, and soup dates. We kept each other company when Ry was in Dubai for 15 months and got to know each other very well; I loved hearing all about Laura's life experiences along with the cutest of stories about Ryan from when he was little. My favorite was when she asked him for a hug and he, just a young toddler, responded, "I don't have any more, but if you wait just an eentsy teentsy minute, I'll make some more in my heart." Laura teaches me things every time we are together – from business to relationships to lessons in the kitchen. She is famous for her colorful fruit salads, perfectly grilled sweet potatoes, and the best roasted chicken (though I still have never had the pleasure to taste it!). When the days were short and cold, she would whip up the quintessential winter soup. After a brisk winter walk, we would un-bundle and sit down together, warming up with two hot bowls of beef stew. Every time I make it, I think of her and all of our special times together. When given the task, she picked out two bowls for the book and couldn't decide which one to choose – I chose the red one for her because it is vibrant, calming, and full of love all in one.

INGREDIENTS:

Serves: 6

Prep time:
15 minutes

Cook time:
6-12 hours

- 2 lb. beef round cubes
- 4+ cups beef stock
- 3 medium carrots, chopped
- 4 stalks celery, chopped
- 1 large parsnip, chopped
- 2 cups mushrooms, chopped
- 1 onion, chopped
- 4 plum tomatoes, chopped
- 1 Tbsp. garlic, chopped
- 1 tsp. oregano
- 1 tsp. sage
- 1 tsp. thyme
- 1 tsp. onion powder
- 1 tsp. parsley
- 1 bay leaf
- 1 tsp. salt
- 1 tsp. pepper

INSTRUCTIONS:

1 / **Add all ingredients to crockpot.**

2 / **Cook for 10-12 hours on low or 6-7 hours on high.**

G.I.T. SWEET POTATO BISQUE
FOR KATE MAURER-HOLLAENDER

In high school and college, many girls have names for their groups of friends (think the Queen Bees and Wannabees in *Mean Girls*). In college, Kate and I were no different as proud G.I.T.s, or Grandmas in Training. We wore our name loud and proud, cherishing cozy dinners at home watching *Law and Order: Special Victims Unit* marathons in our pajamas. We'd cook outrageously large meals for Pi Phi chapter dinners, feeding nearly 200 people in a night. One time I put together my first "cookbook" that consisted of all of our friends' and suitemates' favorite recipes, which Kate lovingly reminded me of recently. Instead of the campus cafeteria, we ate nearly all of our meals at the local Bread & Company, and when we were feeling dangerous we'd venture to Maggie Moo's for an ice cream concoction with all of our favorite toppings. The only thing that has ever stood in the way of our dining is the tickle sessions I'd subject Kate to, seeing as she is literally the most ticklish person I know. Though she claims to hate it, her husband and I are convinced she can't live without a good tickle session, complete with rolling laughter and squealing for dear life. I stood by Kate's side as her bridesmaid when she married her college sweetheart, and I will always be her fellow G.I.T. Kate gave me a lovely white and pink bowl which was the perfect vessel for a cozy, winter, G.I.T. soup.

INGREDIENTS:

INSTRUCTIONS:

Serves: 4

Prep time:
15 minutes

Cook time:
60 minutes

Tip:
Substitute some of the sweet potatoes (up to half) with carrots to lower the carbohydrates and glycemic index of this soup. You will also get some additional nutrients, like beta-carotene and vitamin A!

1 ½ Tbsp. olive or coconut oil

2 large sweet onions, chopped

2 Tbsp. garlic, chopped

½ tsp. sea salt

¼ tsp. pepper

4 medium or 6 small sweet potatoes, peeled & cubed

4 cups chicken stock or water

8 oz. full-fat coconut milk

½ cup coconut flakes, unsweetened & lightly toasted

1 / Heat oil over medium heat in a large soup pot.

2 / Add onions, garlic, sea salt, and pepper, and cook for 10 minutes, stirring often.

3 / Add sweet potatoes and cook for another 10 minutes, stirring often.

4 / Add stock or water and bring to a boil.

5 / When it boils, simmer covered over medium-low heat for 30 minutes.

6 / Let the soup cool for a few minutes.

7 / Purée the soup until smooth.

8 / Add the coconut milk and stir until well combined.

9 / Top with lightly toasted coconut flakes.

MALAWIAN CHICKEN CURRY SWEET POTATO STEW

<u>FOR</u> A.J. WALKLEY

A.J. and I met in elementary school, and reconnected over the past few years thanks to the incredible novels she has written and her interest in my SoooPaleo blog. It has been wonderful getting to know each other again as adults. While a bit different from our days selling Samoas and Thin Mints with the Trumbull Brownie Girl Scout Troop, and smearing pats of butter onto dinner rolls from the Holiday Hill Day Camp cafeteria in between talent show practices, she is still the same kind soul with an incredible heart. In reality, this whole book exists because she suggested that I turn my blog into a cookbook. She helped build my confidence to turn a longtime dream into a reality, and I will never be able to repay her for that. She has answered hundreds of my questions relating to writing, publishing, and Kickstarter, and I truly wouldn't have gotten through the roller coaster without her. I am so thrilled to say she is my esteemed editor and one of the purest examples of a true friend that I have ever found. A.J. held her own Kickstarter for her novel, *Vuto*, and one of the rewards for her backers was a traditional Malawian meal of curried chicken, representing the Indian influences that have come into the African nation. That being the case, there was no better choice for her soup than this.

INGREDIENTS:

INSTRUCTIONS:

Serves: 4

Prep time:
10 minutes

Cook time:
45 minutes

2 Tbsp. coconut oil

1 tsp. ground cumin

1 tsp. ground turmeric

1 Tbsp. curry powder

1 large onion, chopped

Coarse salt & freshly
ground black pepper to taste

2 Tbsp. fresh ginger, minced

4 cloves garlic, minced

2 medium sweet potatoes,
peeled & diced

1 red bell pepper, chopped

1 lb. boneless, skinless chicken

4 cups vegetable or chicken stock

6 oz. coconut milk (optional)

Fresh cilantro, chopped (optional)

1 / Heat oil over medium heat.

2 / Add spices and cook for 1-2 minutes until fragrant.

3 / Add onion, salt, and pepper, and cook 5-10 minutes until soft.

4 / Add ginger and garlic, and cook 2 more minutes.

5 / Add sweet potatoes and bell pepper, and cook 1 minute.

6 / Add chicken and stock, and bring to a boil.

7 / Cover, reduce heat to medium-low, and simmer for 30 minutes.

8 / Remove chicken, shred or chop, and return it to the pot.

9 / If you prefer a creamier or thicker stew, add coconut milk and stir well to combine.

10 / Finish it off with fresh cilantro on top.

PURÉE OF PURPLE
FOR SARAH BOWLING

Sarah and I have known each other for about 10 years, and she is the only beautiful math geek I know that could become the next Martha Stewart. Sarah was my only real friend in the math department at Vanderbilt, going on to become my colleague and neighbor in Stamford. We cooked countless meals together and would eat our dinner on the living room floor of my first apartment watching episodes of *The Biggest Loser*. As we moved on to nicer apartments and better meals, we had several life-altering conversations around the kitchen island about the men we love, difficult career decisions, engagement rings, and dream homes; we always had our best chats at the kitchen counter. We have had our fair share of memories, including the time we ran 10 blocks in torrential rain through Manhattan to get to a family dinner party, only to step in a 12-inch puddle of standing water right outside the restaurant. Sarah, bent over and hysterical, "had an accident" that made me follow suit, leading to a sopping wet dinner experience for the two of us, in more ways than one. Sarah told me that I have always been a hostess at heart, constantly making sure my guests are well fed. Even when I had surgery on my finger in college, and was completely dazed from anesthesia and pain killers, I greeted her at the door of my suite, offering her sandwiches and sweets. The truth is that I have always looked up to Sarah's values, and I am counting down until we can be wives and mothers together to share recipes, swap gross stories, and pick up the phone for a good laugh or cry together. As one of my best friends on Earth, there are many things that remind me of Sarah, but most of all is her favorite color. It's an assurance I will always think of Sarah when I make the following dish, inspired by her love of all things purple.

INGREDIENTS:

INSTRUCTIONS:

Serves: 4

Prep time:
15 minutes

Cook time:
55 minutes

1 Tbsp. olive oil

1 Tbsp. garlic, chopped

1 sweet onion, chopped

1 leek (whites only), sliced

2 stalks celery, chopped

1 yellow squash, chopped

1 bunch purple (or white) asparagus, chopped

1 head purple cauliflower, chopped

4 cups vegetable or chicken stock

Cracked black pepper (optional)

Fresh rosemary (optional)

1 / Heat oil over medium heat.

2 / Sauté the garlic, onion, and leek about 10 minutes until soft.

3 / Add the celery, squash, and asparagus, and cook another 5 minutes.

4 / Add the cauliflower and stock, and bring to a boil.

5 / Simmer covered over medium-low heat for 40 minutes or until veggies are soft.

6 / Let the soup cool for a few minutes and then purée until smooth.

7 / Serve with black cracked pepper and fresh rosemary.

MOROCCAN LAMB TAGINE
FOR JOANNA PIETRI

- -

Throughout my whole childhood, I dreamt of having a foreign exchange student I could show around, swap stories with, and through whom I could gain access to another world. In June of 2003, my prayers were answered when my dad told me that we were going to have a French girl my same age stay with us in Nashville for the summer. From the minute Joanna arrived, we were like long-lost sisters living parallel lives across the pond. I felt badly that Joanna was at a disadvantage speaking English, so we would stay up late at night speaking Spanish to each other, on an even level with one another since we were both searching for our words. We spent every minute together that summer, and I was single-handedly responsible for introducing her to every American food, shopping experience, and tradition. When her family returned the favor the following summer and hosted me in St. Tropez, she took me to the outdoor market where I must have sampled a dozen French pastries and the freshest fruits; my favorite, however, was the Polish cream cake dubbed the "Tropezienne Tart": velvety cream sandwiched between layers of incredibly pillowy brioche cakes, topped with a generous helping of thick sugar crystals. Between every bite, Joanna would exclaim, "Mmmm!" just like she did at every meal we shared together. It has been over a decade since we met, and we have joined one another all around the world, tasting our way through new cities, and forging memories that will last a lifetime. Our next adventure will hopefully take place in Morocco, making Joanna's soup particularly apropos.

INGREDIENTS:

INSTRUCTIONS:

- -

Serves: 6

Prep time:
15 minutes

Cook time:
8-10 hours

2 medium onions, sliced

4 carrots, peeled & chopped

Water

2 lb. lamb shoulder (can also use lamb shank or leg of lamb)

Sea salt & pepper

2 Tbsp. lamb spice mix (rosemary, rose petals, cumin, paprika, onion powder, garlic powder, mint)

2 Tbsp. garlic, chopped

1 Tbsp. fresh rosemary

8 matchstick slices ginger, 1-inch each

1 cup dried apricots

1 ½ cups prunes

1 / Lay onions and carrots at the bottom of the crockpot.

2 / Cover with water (just enough to barely cover).

3 / Lightly season the lamb with sea salt and pepper.

4 / Spice both sides of the lamb with the spice mixture, and then lay it on top of the onions and carrots.

5 / Make a few slits in the lamb, and stuff with chopped garlic and rosemary.

6 / Add the ginger, apricots, and prunes to the crockpot.

7 / Cover and cook on low for 8-10 hours.

8 / Remove the ginger, shred the lamb, and serve!

GOD ALMIGHTY, NICE CAULIFLOWER
FOR DANIELLE SEESTED

I absolutely worshipped my cousin Danni when I was a little girl. As the youngest cousin in our family, I looked up to everyone – both literally and figuratively – but I counted down the days until I could see Danni again, try on her clothes, and hear her stories. She gave me some pretty fantastic velvet hand-me-downs over the years, and taught me about boys, "cool" music (like Savage Garden), and girls-only secrets. On a visit to my house in Connecticut as kids, we went pumpkin picking and came up with the phrase, "God almighty, nice pumpkins!" – a saying that immediately stuck and we've used in all sorts of situations since; we still compliment each other's "pumpkins" to this day.

While this is not a pumpkin-based soup, the ingredients remind me of cool afternoons on the cusp of winter, admiring Danni as I followed her around, and learned from my role model cousin.

INGREDIENTS:

INSTRUCTIONS:

Serves: 4

Prep time:
10 minutes

Cook time:
45 minutes

1 head cauliflower, halved, cored, & cut into florets

3 Tbsp. olive oil, divided

1 head garlic

1 white onion, chopped

4 cups chicken stock or water

½ tsp. salt

¼ tsp. white pepper

1 / Preheat oven to 375 degrees.

2 / Toss cauliflower with 1 ½ Tbsp. of the oil and arrange on a baking sheet.

3 / Prep the garlic by removing the extra paper, cutting off the top ¼-inch of the head, and brushing the exposed cloves with ½ Tbsp. oil. Wrap it in foil and then add it to the baking sheet with the cauliflower.

4 / Roast for 20 minutes until lightly golden brown.

5 / Meanwhile, heat the remaining 1 Tbsp. of oil over medium heat.

6 / Add the onion and cook 5-10 minutes until soft, but not brown.

7 / Add the cauliflower, garlic cloves, and stock or water.

8 / Bring to a boil and then simmer covered over medium-low heat for about 15 minutes, until cauliflower is very soft.

9 / Purée the soup, and season with salt and pepper to serve.

PEPPERY BEETS, SWEETS, & KALE
FOR SANJIDA KARIM

Sanjida was my first friend in Stamford at my first job out of college. Though we were on separate teams at work, she immediately stepped in to show me the ropes. One of the kindest people I know, we have stayed close through many job changes and moves all around the world. You all have a lot to thank Sanjida for because, before her, I barely even used salt or pepper when cooking, let alone other spices. For Sanjida, this was tantamount to sacrilege considering that I've never seen her eat a single meal without a solid helping of hot sauce or pepper covering the dish. I would cook dinner for the two of us all the time after work and had to buy a special pepper shaker just for her to cover her meal with before she ate. Over the years I finally gave in and now I actually love spice in my food – the more flavor the better! Ironically, Sanjida sent me a note recently telling me that she appreciated how all of my old dishes were so simple and taught her that she didn't always need to flavor her food with a million different spices. She learned that simple, healthy, and fresh ingredients went a long way, even without the pepper! Hopefully Sanjida will agree that the soups in this book are all seasoned just right, with or without the extra spice. For her soup, I chose one with simple, raw ingredients and the opportunity for lots of flavor!

INGREDIENTS:

INSTRUCTIONS:

Serves: 3

Prep time:
15 minutes

Cook time:
70 minutes

1 Tbsp. olive oil

1 sweet onion, chopped

5 cloves garlic, chopped

1 large beet, peeled & chopped

4 cups vegetable stock

1 large sweet potato, peeled & chopped

1 bunch kale, cut into 1-inch pieces

Generous sprinkle of salt & freshly ground black pepper to taste

1 / Heat oil over medium heat.

2 / Add onion and garlic, and cook for at least **10 minutes until soft and lightly browned.**

3 / Add beet and stock, and bring to a boil.

4 / Cover and simmer over medium heat for **30 minutes, then add sweet potato.**

5 / Cook another **20-25 minutes** covered until the sweet potatoes are soft.

6 / Add kale.

7 / Cook for an additional **5 minutes,** and then serve with salt and pepper to taste. **The longer you cook it, the sweeter it will be!**

TOPAZ GREEN GODDESS SOUP
FOR KARA SALVAGNO

As my next-door neighbor on Topaz Lane, and the mother of my childhood best friend, Steph, Kara was always a second mom to me. We met in 1989 and have shared countless memories since. As a child, I would cherish sleepovers at Steph's so I could eat Kara's French toast sticks with real Vermont maple syrup (we only had low-fat Bisquick and sugar-free Aunt Jemima syrup in our house!). Kara and I would bake cookies during snow days, and experiment with soups in the kitchen.

Kara told me that if I were to use the bowls of soup as a metaphor for life, she would guess that her bowl would represent the collective neighborhood that we dwelled in. The chicken stock would be the milieu that brought us all together into a cohesive, united, friendly unit; all of the veggies would represent the individuals that make up the collective "soup." She would like to think that she represents the red pepper flavor burst that kicks it up a notch. Alternatively, she said that we may think of her as the wilted spinach – a dried up, soggy, old, retired woman living in the remote desert, and that's okay, too.

INGREDIENTS:

INSTRUCTIONS:

Serves: 4

Prep time:
10 minutes

Cook time:
45 minutes

Tip:
The beauty of this soup is that you can throw anything in – empty your fridge and throw the veggies in the pot (the more green, the better)! I used to call this recipe "Garbage Soup" as a result, but thought that "Green Goddess" was a bit more tempting!

8 cups chicken stock

1 bag spinach leaves

1 bunch kale, roughly chopped

1 handful cabbage, chopped

1 green zucchini, chopped

3 carrots, peeled & chopped

3 stalks celery, chopped

1 onion, chopped

**1 pinch garlic powder
or minced garlic**

**½ tsp. cayenne pepper
(or more to taste)**

Broccoli, chopped (optional)

Asparagus, chopped (optional)

1 / **Add all ingredients to a large soup pot and bring to a boil.**

2 / **Cover and simmer over medium-low heat for 30 minutes or until all vegetables are soft.**

3 / **Purée soup until frothy and smooth.**

SAN FRANCISO BUFFALO CHILI
FOR BRIDGETT LUTHER & TIM AHERN

A colleague of my dad's who felt drawn to the *Bowls of Love* message, Bridgett was adamant about how connected she feels to others through the power of food and cooking. On the last Saturday every January, she and her husband, Tim, host a chili party to start the year off right for all of their friends and loved ones. The annual "abundance" party has the underlying theme that there is enough to go around for everyone if they just take the time to stop and enjoy it. The day is always simple, focusing on enjoying what they have, including each other. Every attendee arrives, bowl in hand, and heads straight to the dueling pots on the stove. Chili is a dish almost everyone likes, which is why it was chosen for the event. Accents for the dish are offered in the form of diced onions, cheese, a variety of peppers, and Fritos to make "Chili Pie" – one of the most popular ways their guests have discovered to consume this family favorite. Their guest list continues to grow, year-by-year, and I am fortunate enough to have garnered a standing invitation to this culinary event! Their daughter, Kalle, now with two boys of her own, has started the next generation of chili-goers. With such a beautiful tradition based on family, friends, and food, there was no question about which soup I'd make for Bridgett and Tim.

INGREDIENTS:

Serves: 6-8

Prep time:
15 minutes

Cook time:
45 minutes

1-2 Tbsp. coconut oil

2 onions, diced

3 cloves garlic, minced

2 lb. ground buffalo

(1) 28 oz. can tomatoes, diced

1 cup tomato sauce

(1) 4 oz. can green chilies

1 cup beef stock

1 Tbsp. chili powder

2 Tbsp. cumin

1 yellow bell pepper, diced

1 red bell pepper, diced

Sea salt & freshly ground black pepper to taste

¼ cup cilantro (optional)

2 scallions (optional)

1 avocado (optional)

INSTRUCTIONS:

1 / Heat oil over medium heat.

2 / Add onions and cook for 5 minutes.

3 / Add garlic and ground buffalo, and stir, breaking up large pieces with a spoon.

4 / When meat is fully cooked (5-7 minutes), stir in tomatoes, tomato sauce, chilies, beef stock, chili powder, and cumin.

5 / Adjust temperature so that the liquids aren't splattering everywhere, but keeping the heat as high as possible.

6 / Leave the lid off to simmer so the chili can thicken up. Simmer for at least 30 minutes so the spices absorb into the meat.

7 / After the chili thickens, stir in chopped bell peppers, and adjust seasoning with salt and pepper. Add more chili pepper if you like it hot!

8 / Serve with chopped cilantro, scallions, and avocado as garnishes.

WOODEN PIG CARNITAS
FOR KEVIN RAYNES

Kevin and I started our careers at McLagan on the exact same day. Three years his senior, I was chosen as his mentor, and we have spent many lunches and dinners together plotting our world domination ever since. Before I moved to Boston, we used to have mentor lunches at Tengda, a little Asian café in downtown Stamford. We exclusively ordered the enormous lunch specials with teriyaki salmon, salad, veggies, and more – a veritable smorgasbord of food that left us with full bellies and happy taste buds. I always customized the California Roll to include brown rice and mango, and Kevin would begrudgingly agree to share as long as he could get the pan-fried gyoza; I had to relent. As his mentor, I have tried to teach Kevin organization, prioritization, and how to complete tasks more efficiently. I may or may not have had to remind him five times about providing a bowl for this project, but it turns out that patience pays off! Kevin officially wins the Most Creative Bowl Award. Little did he know that I had already planned to make pork carnitas for his soup, and he provided the most perfect wooden pig to hold it in.

INGREDIENTS:

INSTRUCTIONS:

Serves: 8-12

Prep time:
10 minutes

Cook time:
4-10 hours

2 large onions, sliced

10 cloves garlic, chopped

4 lb. pork loin roast (can also use pork shoulder or pork butt), trimmed of excess fat

4 bay leaves

1 Tbsp. cumin

1 Tbsp. paprika

1 Tbsp. oregano

1 Tbsp. cinnamon

1 Tbsp. onion powder

1 Tbsp. garlic powder

1 tsp. salt

½ tsp. pepper

¼ tsp. cayenne pepper

2 cups cherry tomatoes

2 cups vegetable stock or water

1 / Lay onions and garlic in the bottom of the crockpot.

2 / Season the pork very generously with all seasonings on both sides.

3 / Lay the pork on top of the onions, fat side up.

4 / Add cherry tomatoes and stock or water.

5 / Cook on low for 8-10 hours or on high for 4-6 hours.

6 / Shred the pork with kitchen tongs or a pair of forks, and stir so the juices mix. Keep warm in the crockpot, and serve in your favorite wooden pig!

BIG BERTHA'S ITALIAN WEDDING SOUP
FOR STEPHANIE SALVAGNO

At the lucky age of four, my family moved to Topaz Lane in Connecticut and joined the best neighborhood in America – or at least one of them. Our house was at the top of a huge hill and on the very first day there, I drove my pink Barbie Corvette convertible off the moving truck, down the long driveway, and right across the street to my neighbor's house. When the door opened, my new best friend was standing there, and the rest is history. Steph is my oldest friend; we have spent a quarter of a century by each other's sides and our friendship has a solid foundation unlike any other. We have truly gone through everything together; from our annual epic block parties, to our first pair of red socks, to life-altering crushes on the Backstreet Boys, we grew and matured together over the years. Though I was more focused on shopping when Steph was swimming and playing sports, we always managed to find common ground. As Steph says, "I have never, and will never, have a friend that has known me for so long and so well." Steph and I have a dozen nicknames for each other (Berta, Bertha, Camel, Zebra...), so the zebra bowl is a perfect representation of our love and friendship. The soup is particularly appropriate because I cannot wait to be by her side for all of the wonderful adventures ahead, especially one certain occasion...

INGREDIENTS:

INSTRUCTIONS:

Serves: 4

Prep time:
20 minutes

Cook time:
1 hour

Meatballs:
1 lb. grass-fed ground beef

2 Tbsp. almond flour

1 tsp. garlic powder

1 tsp. Italian seasoning

Dash of salt & pepper

Soup:
1 Tbsp. olive oil

1 medium onion

1 Tbsp. garlic, chopped

3 stalks celery, chopped

2 medium carrots, chopped

1 pint cherry tomatoes, halved

4 cups chicken or beef stock

1 Tbsp. Italian seasoning

1 tsp. salt

½ tsp. pepper

1 bunch kale, chopped

1 / **Mix all meatball ingredients thoroughly and roll into 1-inch balls (should make about 16).**

2 / **Heat oil over medium heat.**

3 / **Add meatballs and cook for a few minutes on all sides until lightly browned.**

4 / **Remove meatballs and set aside.**

5 / **Add onion, garlic, celery, and carrots to the meatball drippings, and cook for 10 minutes until soft.**

6 / **Add meatballs, tomatoes, stock, Italian seasoning, salt, and pepper, and bring to a boil.**

7 / **Cover and simmer over medium-low heat for 40 minutes.**

8 / **Add chopped kale leaves and cook for additional 5 minutes until kale is wilted.**

ZUPPA TOSCANA

<u>FOR</u> KARL ROBE

- -

Another one of my dad's colleagues, Karl was eager to support this cookbook, being personally connected to the *Bowls of Love* message. He believes that food engages our senses and transports us; a simple whiff or glimpse for Karl brings back memories of childhood comforts and momentous life events, whether happy or sad. Food provides sustenance physically, mentally, and emotionally. Food strengthens. Food excites with new experiences. Food grounds us in tradition. From his mother's kitchen to his own today, food has been and always will be part of the journey. Karl's wife and children are his favorite dining companions; he fondly told me about great memories eating Zuppa Toscana at Olive Garden with his family by his side.

With his love of that dish in mind, I whipped up a fresh, Paleo-inspired version for him and his family to try.

INGREDIENTS:

INSTRUCTIONS:

- -

Serves: 4-6

Prep time:
15 minutes

Cook time:
40 minutes

Did You Know
that there are two types of sweet potatoes? One has copper skin and orange flesh (often confused with yams), and the other has golden skin with white creamy flesh (like the one in this recipe!).

1 Tbsp. olive oil

1 lb. chicken sausage, casing removed

1 medium onion, diced

4 cloves garlic, minced

8 cups chicken stock

1 medium turnip, peeled & chopped

1 medium parsnip, peeled & chopped

1 medium sweet potato, peeled & chopped

1 large bunch kale, stems removed

1 cup almond milk (optional)

Salt & pepper to taste

1 / **Heat oil over medium heat.**

2 / **Add chicken sausage and cook until browned, about 10 minutes.**

3 / **Add onion and garlic, and cook another 5 minutes, stirring frequently.**

4 / **Add stock, turnip, parsnip, and sweet potato, and bring to a boil.**

5 / **Cover, reduce heat to low, and simmer for 15-20 minutes until veggies are soft.**

6 / **Add kale and almond milk (if desired), and simmer another 5 minutes uncovered until kale is wilted.**

7 / **Add salt and pepper to taste.**

SPRING

REBELLIOUS SPRING PURÉE WITH CRISP BACON
FOR EVAN RAKOWSKI

If you ask my older brother, Evan, about my favorite childhood snack, he would say his Nintendo controllers. I prefer to disagree, since I can neither confirm nor deny that I used to chew on the controller cords while I watched him play his video games. As my palate has matured over the years, Evan and I shared countless family meals together, and my eating habits continued to annoy. I used to be a very slow eater and he wasn't allowed to leave the table until I finished. Thirty minutes into a Dunkin' Donuts banana nut muffin, and I would have barely made any progress. Luckily, I have reached a normal eating speed and Evan now teaches me all about the best food New York City has to offer. He has fed me the hands-down best bagels; biggest, most ridiculous cookies; cow-sized steaks; and the most absurdly delicious, face-swallowing waffles.

Considering just how many of my favorite culinary treats he's introduced me to over the years, I guess it's time to admit that, fine, okay Evan, I chewed the wires... forgive me? Thinking that rubber wire soup wouldn't entice my readers, I went a different route. While a strict Paleo diet avoids peas (and all other legumes), I had to include one rebellious recipe for my brother with the freshest picked English peas from the garden. Only ripe and available for a few weeks every year, these peas remind me of childhood trips to Stew Leonard's and pair perfectly with the crisp bacon. Served in your beautiful, hand-picked bowl, this one's for you, big brother.

INGREDIENTS:

Serves: 4

Prep time:
10 minutes

Cook time:
30 minutes

4 oz. bacon (3-4 strips)

2 leeks (whites and greens), sliced (about 2 cups)

1 Tbsp. garlic, chopped

3 cups English peas, shelled

4 cups vegetable stock or water

6 oz. spinach

Salt & white pepper to taste

INSTRUCTIONS:

1 / Cook bacon in a skillet on the stovetop or on a baking sheet for **15-20 minutes at 400 degrees** until crisp.

2 / When crisp, remove bacon to a plate lined with paper towel.

3 / Discard all but 1 tsp. of the bacon grease.

4 / Heat the grease over medium heat.

5 / Add leeks and garlic, and cook for **10 minutes.**

6 / Add peas and stock, bringing to a boil for **5 minutes** until peas are tender.

7 / Add spinach, cover, and cook **2-3 additional minutes** until wilted.

8 / Purée soup, add salt and pepper to taste, and serve immediately topped with crumbled bacon.

ALL-AMERICAN HAMBURGER DELUXE
FOR BRITTANI BOBOWICK

Thanks to a little luck when I really needed it, Brittani became my roommate in a beautiful two-story house in Cambridge, right in the heart of Inman Square. Brittani and I shared a lot of things in common, everything from Bikram yoga to men – her husband, Trevor, was one of my first boyfriends when I was only 13 years old! I cannot think of Brittani without ice cream coming to mind in the same thought, as this is one true love we both share. We loved either walking down the street past the exotic spice market to Christina's Homemade Ice Cream where we would sample flavors like burnt sugar, fresh rose, and honey lavender; or running to the corner store on a rainy night before cuddling up on the couch together with a pint of Ben & Jerry's and two spoons. We would take turns savoring our dessert while we caught up on life's latest gossip...and stalked my next potential online date. When we weren't indulging, I would teach her about new foods and cooking techniques as I whipped up delicious meals for the two of us after Brittani's long commute home from the office. In return, she taught me how she became the perfect Southern belle, complete with rollers in her hair. An all-American Texan sweetheart, Brittani deserved a soup that speaks to her meat and potatoes mentality.

INGREDIENTS:

Serves: 4

Prep time:
15 minutes

Cook time:
70 minutes

6 slices bacon

1 lb. organic, grass-fed ground beef

1 medium onion, sliced

2 cloves garlic, minced

2 cups mushrooms, chopped

1 tsp. dried parsley

1 tsp. dried basil

4 cups vegetable or beef stock

1 tsp. salt

½ tsp. pepper

Avocado (optional)

INSTRUCTIONS:

1 / Preheat oven to 400 degrees.

2 / Put bacon on a foil-lined baking sheet and bake for about 15-20 minutes, turning once, until crispy.

3 / Meanwhile, cook the ground beef in a soup pot with a pinch of salt and pepper until cooked through (about 8-10 minutes).

4 / Drain fat from the pot and set the meat aside.

5 / Add onion and garlic to pot with the meat drippings, and cook over medium-high heat until onions start to caramelize (about 20-25 minutes).

6 / Add mushrooms, herbs, stock, salt, and pepper to pot and bring to a boil.

7 / Simmer uncovered over medium-low heat for 20 minutes.

8 / Crumble bacon and add bacon pieces along with ground beef into the soup.

9 / Top with avocado or your favorite burger topping, and serve with some delicious baked sweet potato fries!

TRUFFLED ASPARAGUS MUGS OF LOVE
FOR VIKKI ROZIER

Every second that goes by in my life, I find myself becoming more and more like my mom. I always said I would never say things like "gallivanting around town" or "dillydallying" but, alas, the inevitable has happened. As you know by now, I spent countless hours watching my mom's every move in the kitchen while I was growing up. Desperate to help her, I was typically only allowed to do the boring tasks like setting the table. She nicknamed me "Helpful Hannah" because every time I tried to help, it was a certainty that a giant catastrophe was on the horizon. Once, I insisted that I wanted to be her assistant and help carry the groceries upstairs; all was well until I dropped a full gallon of milk on the tile floor. The plastic broke and the entire gallon spread throughout the kitchen, under the fridge, and between the grout; needless to say, Hannah was not invited to help the next time.

To this day, though there are over 1,000 miles between us, our relationship is unlike any other; we talk on the phone at least three times a day, and I really do believe we are an extension of each other. She has been by my side through every single celebration and disaster (there have been many of both!), filling my soul with the strongest tough love on the planet. There isn't a single other human on this planet I am more proud of for everything she's accomplished as a mother and woman. Mom gave me two mugs for her recipe so we could eat together, and each one came with a matching plate to catch the inevitable spills. While the plates didn't make the photo, the mugs of love will forever remind me of our close bond, frightening similarities, and enormous capacity for love.

INGREDIENTS:

Serves: 4

Prep time:
10 minutes

Cook time:
35 minutes

1 Tbsp. olive oil

2 shallots, chopped

1 onion, chopped

1 Tbsp. garlic, chopped

2 lb. asparagus, chopped

½ tsp. salt

¼ tsp. white pepper

4 cups vegetable stock or water

Truffle oil (optional)

Truffle salt (optional)

INSTRUCTIONS:

1 / Heat oil over medium heat.

2 / Add shallots, onion, and garlic, and cook for 10 minutes.

3 / Add asparagus, salt, and pepper, and cook for another 3-4 minutes.

4 / Add stock, bring to a boil, and simmer covered over medium-low heat for 20 minutes.

5 / Remove from heat, purée, and top with truffle oil and a pinch of truffle salt.

RUSTIC SHRIMP BISQUE
FOR AUSTIN RAKOWSKI

My look-alike younger brother, Austin, is the reason my *Bowls of Love* Kickstarter campaign was such a success. At only 16 years old, Austin directed, filmed, and perfected my video for the world to see. He is known for many other famous videos in our family, including a few submissions into our annual Christmas cookie competition. All family members have to bake a cookie and present it to the judging panel to be rated on taste, presentation, and creativity. Austin's presentations almost always rank above the rest, but he has yet to win given the unmistakable soap taste in all of his cookies. We've never known exactly why, considering that it's unlikely Austin even washes his hands before crafting his contest entries, let alone come in contact with enough soap to ruin the batter. Regardless of his skills (or lack thereof) in the kitchen, Austin has held a special place in my life from the minute he was born. When my dad told me he was going to have more children, I said it was fine with me as long as he didn't have another daughter; he went on to have twin boys. I could not have been happier with the new siblings that I was blessed with, and I am so proud of the man Austin is becoming. He has an amazing sense of humor, a creative mind, and a sensitive heart of gold that I will forever nourish and respect.

Austin was one of the lucky few who were allowed to see my draft recipe list for this cookbook before I cooked or assigned them to anyone specifically. He chose this soup himself, knowing how lovely it would look in his rustic bowl – a planter from Terrain, a garden oasis in Westport, CT.

INGREDIENTS:

Serves: 4

Prep time:
15 minutes

Cook time:
40 minutes

1 Tbsp. oil

1 large carrot, chopped

3 stalks celery, chopped

1 red bell pepper, chopped

1 onion, chopped

(1) 6 oz. can coconut milk

1 cup tomato sauce

2 cups water

2 tsp. Old Bay seasoning

1 lb. peeled & deveined shrimp
with tails on

INSTRUCTIONS:

1 / Heat oil over medium heat.

2 / Sauté carrot, celery, bell pepper, and onion for 20 minutes, stirring frequently.

3 / Add coconut milk, tomato sauce, water, and Old Bay, and bring to a boil.

4 / Boil 10 minutes or until vegetables soften.

5 / Add shrimp and simmer covered over medium-low heat for 5 minutes.

6 / Remove shrimp from pot, discard the tails, and chop the shrimp.

7 / Add half of the chopped shrimp back to the pot, and purée until smooth.

8 / Add the remaining chopped shrimp to the bisque, or save to use as a garnish.

CHILLED "BOOM" SOUP WITH MARYLAND CRAB

FOR JULIA ZIMMERMAN

Julia, my cousin Adam's wife, is one of the sweetest people I know who exudes love to everyone she meets. The couple met on eHarmony.com and were such a special pair that they were chosen to be in one of the website's commercials. Julia stole the show, telling viewers, "When I met Adam, it was like BOOM!" Julia has yet to live that comment down, with friends and family still calling her just to say "Boom!" to this day. Living outside of D.C. with their daughter, Ella, I take notes from Julia on how to be a wonderful wife and mother. Despite the fact that I didn't end up finding my true love on eHarmony (though we all know I tried!), I hope to follow in Julia's footsteps in other ways as I become a wife, and one day a mom.

This recipe was designed for her and her family to make when the Maryland crab is fresh to start spring with a boom!

INGREDIENTS:

Serves: 4

Prep time:
20 minutes

Chill time:
4+ hours

2 orange bell peppers, chopped (about 1 ½ cups)

2 cucumbers, peeled, seeded, & chopped (about 3 cups)

2 cups honeydew melon, chopped

¼ medium red onion, diced

½ small jalapeño, seeded & chopped

2 Tbsp. olive oil, divided

1 Tbsp. fresh lemon juice

1 tsp. fine sea salt

½ lb. lump crab meat

½ tsp. sherry vinegar

Salt & pepper to taste

2 green onions, chopped

INSTRUCTIONS:

1 / Purée bell peppers, cucumbers, honeydew, onion, jalapeño, 1 Tbsp. oil, lemon juice, and salt in a blender or food processor.

2 / Chill in refrigerator for at least 4 hours (overnight is best).

3 / Before serving, toss crab with remaining 1 Tbsp. olive oil, sherry vinegar, and salt and pepper to taste.

4 / Serve cold soup topped with crab and green onions.

NORTH STAR MUSHROOM PURÉE
FOR MELINDA MARTINO

Unlike her sister, Mallory, Melinda is a skilled baker. I would expect nothing less of someone who has a dedicated craft room, but Melinda can create the best cookies, brownies, and dipped pretzels you can imagine. Each time she shares them, they are presented beautifully in decorative wrapping, tied into perfect little gifts with handcurled ribbons. Melinda is the little sister I never had — she lovingly lets me be the crazy adopted daughter in the Martino family, and always includes me and treats me like one of the crew. We grew close when she visited me in Boston and I took her to my neighborhood Italian restaurant, City Girl Café, for a night of mouthwatering eats and therapeutic conversation. Melin took her bowl responsibility very seriously and personally hand painted this bowl for me. I was so honored and excited to receive it in the mail knowing all of the thought and effort that went into its creation. Her soup is inspired by one of our favorite local restaurants, North Star in Pound Ridge, NY. The executive chef, Franz Fruhmann, is a culinary genius who creates two heavenly soups every night (almost always Paleo!) that have the whole restaurant raving. The owner, David Schlack, was nice enough to invite me into their kitchen to experience the behind the-scenes secrets that go into their farm-to-table creations. The recipe is now here for all of you to enjoy! Sadly, I forgot that the only food Melinda dislikes is mushrooms — I hope she forgives me for filling her beautiful bowl with her least favorite food!

INGREDIENTS:

INSTRUCTIONS:

Serves: 8-10

Prep time:
15 minutes

Cook time:
35 minutes

2 Tbsp. olive oil

6 shallots, peeled & thinly sliced

2 leeks (whites only), thinly sliced

5 lb. white button mushrooms, sliced

1 Tbsp. salt

8 cups water

1 bunch thyme sprigs

3 bay leaves

1 / Heat oil over medium heat.

2 / Add shallots and leeks, and sauté for 5 minutes until soft, but not brown.

3 / Add mushrooms and sauté for 5 minutes

4 / Add salt and sauté another 5 minutes until liquid is released from the mushrooms.

5 / Add water and bring to a boil.

6 / Add thyme and bay leaves, and let soup boil uncovered for 10 minutes.

7 / Turn off the heat and let the soup continue to cook for 10 minutes.

8 / Remove the thyme sprigs and bay leaves.

9 / Purée until smooth and then pour soup through a fine wire mesh strainer.

FLOATING "MATZO" BALL SOUP
FOR AMANDA MOHR

My cousin Amanda and I have two very important things in common: we love the dark meat at Thanksgiving and we are always the last to know about everything that's happening in our family. We formed a pact to tell each other all family news immediately to try and break the cycle, but we still manage to be at the end of the communication trail. When my mom moved down to Florida, Amanda took over the matzo ball soup duties for the family. She learned all the family secrets (like how to get floaters) and has perfected the recipe. One year for Rosh Hashanah I slept over her house in New Jersey and decided to help out. We must have gotten carried away, catching each other up on the latest (not so new) family gossip, which resulted in a completely ruined batch. We measured wrong, only quadrupling a handful of the ingredients, and were left with small, pathetic sinkers. The least I could do was try out a Paleo version for all of my gluten-free friends who need a little dose of Jewish penicillin every now and then. Amanda will notice that her big and beautiful turquoise bamboo bowl is in the background of the photo. I couldn't break the news to her that the bowl had a small hole in it, and every time we tried to photograph the soup, it would leak out all over the table. It now serves as my perfect salad bowl and a gorgeous backdrop for her "matzo" ball soup!

INGREDIENTS:

Serves: 6+

Prep time:
30 minutes

Cook time:
2+ hours

Soup:

**1 medium whole chicken
(about 4 pounds)**

1 large onion, quartered

2 large parsnips, peeled & chopped

1 large turnip, peeled & chopped

2 large carrots, peeled & chopped

1 bunch flat-leaf parsley

1 bunch dill

2 tsp. fine sea salt

Water

Matzo Balls:

4 large eggs

**2 Tbsp. chicken fat,
softened (or olive oil)**

**3 cups almond flour
(from blanched almonds)**

2 tsp. salt, plus more to boil

¼ tsp. pepper

Dash of parsley

INSTRUCTIONS:

Soup:
1 / **Put all of the ingredients in a large soup pot.**
2 / **Cover ingredients with water and bring to a boil.**
3 / **Cover pot and simmer over medium-low heat for at least 2 hours.**
4 / **While the soup is cooking, make the "matzo" balls.**
5 / **When the soup is done, remove the herbs and discard.**
6 / **Remove the chicken from the pot, discard the skin and bones, and add shredded meat back into the pot.**

Matzo Balls:
1 / **Boil large pot of salted water.**
2 / **Beat eggs and melted chicken fat until well combined (at least 1-2 minutes), and set aside.**
3 / **Mix the almond flour, salt, pepper, and parsley.**
4 / **Add the wet ingredients to the dry and mix well until a firm batter is created. If too moist, slowly add additional almond flour until you reach the desired consistency.**
5 / **Cover the mixture and refrigerate for 1 hour.**
6 / **Wet your hands and roll the chilled batter into 1-inch balls (batter should yield 10-12 balls).**
7 / **Carefully drop the balls into the boiling water.**
8 / **Reduce heat and simmer covered over medium-low heat for 30-40 minutes until cooked through.**
9 / **Remove with a slotted spoon and immediately drop the "matzo" balls into the soup.**

SOUS-CHEF CHILLED AJO BLANCO
FOR TARA LERNER

Tara and I were roommates at Vanderbilt junior year in a Towers suite, and senior year in the Pi Phi sorority house. We have our fair share of memories and adventures accumulated over the years, but it is worth noting that she was my original sous-chef. Each week during junior year, Tara and I would go to our local Kroger in Nashville and buy our groceries together like an old married couple. Split down the middle, we would go home and I would cook while Tara chopped and cleaned. It was the perfect marriage (and one everyone should strive for!). Back then, we had our mothers' recipes in mind instead of our own, so we would create the best replicas of my mom's turkey meatballs and Mrs. Lerner's noodle kugel. We were convinced that if we perfected them well enough, one day we would host our own Jewish cooking show on the Food Network. Keep a lookout for us on your TV screen someday soon!

Tara's bowl was hand-picked to highlight the Pi Phi colors, wine and silver blue. I chose this soup knowing that while the title may sound fancy, it is easy enough for my original sous-chef to make!

INGREDIENTS:

INSTRUCTIONS:

Serves: 4

Prep time:
10 minutes

Cook time:
20 minutes

Tip:
Depending on the size of the grapes and cucumbers, you may want to add olive oil, water, and/or vinegar to achieve the desired thickness and taste profile. This soup comes out a bit different every time, but is well worth the experimentation!

3 cloves garlic, pressed

¼ cup leeks (whites only), sliced

1 cup almonds, blanched (plus more to garnish)

¼ cup Spanish olive oil

1-2 Tbsp. sherry vinegar

4 cups green grapes, halved (plus more to garnish)

1 cup cucumber, peeled & chopped

2 cups cold filtered water

2 tsp. salt, plus more to taste

1 / Sauté garlic and leeks over low heat for about 5-7 minutes until soft (do not brown), then move to the fridge to chill.

2 / Combine chilled garlic and leeks with almonds in a food processor or blender.

3 / One at a time, add oil, vinegar, grapes, and cucumber.

4 / Add cold water as needed so the mixture remains smooth as you add ingredients.

5 / Add salt, plus more to taste.

6 / Pour soup through a fine wire-mesh sieve; you will want to rub the sides of the sieve with a rubber spatula to collect as much of the soup as possible. Note: If you like the texture as-is, you can skip this step.

7 / Serve topped with additional olive oil, grapes, and almonds.

EGG DROP SOUP
FOR LAUREN TILLOTSON

I met Lauren in 2011, when I interviewed her for a job on my team at work. We were in a conference room for the interview and I broke out in an absolutely absurd sneezing fit. Unknowingly allergic to her perfume, I was making scrunched faces the whole time, just trying to keep the sneezes in. She was a trooper, we hired her, and she became an absolutely wonderful partner, friend, and "daughter". Lauren and I had a family dinner out at Chocopologie one night before I had to take a train back to Boston, and we must have eaten enough for a football team. Baked brie, short ribs, burgers, and some oh-so indulgent desserts were shared; we could barely walk out of the restaurant! I can always count on her as my foodie buddy, but most importantly through all of the ups and downs in life. She has been by my side as I fell in love and, although she towers over me at 5'9", I promised her she could be the flower girl in my wedding. Her dedication, motivation, and commitment to everything she does helped inspire me to go after my dreams and create *Bowls of Love*. Lauren chose a bowl that was just screaming for an Asian-inspired soup, so I made her a quick and easy high-protein recipe to eat on the run between personal training sessions and Tillotson Twin workouts.

INGREDIENTS:

INSTRUCTIONS:

Serves: 4

Prep time:
10 minutes

Cook time:
15 minutes

Tip:
Feel free to omit the arrowroot powder if you wish — the soup will have the same great taste but will be slightly thinner.

1 Tbsp. olive oil

½ onion, chopped

3 chives, chopped

5 cups chicken stock, divided

⅛ tsp. ground ginger

1 cup mushrooms, chopped

¼ tsp. salt

⅛ tsp. pepper

1 ½ Tbsp. arrowroot powder (optional)

4 eggs

1 / Heat oil over medium heat.

2 / Sauté onion and chives until soft (about 5 minutes).

3 / Add 4 cups of the stock along with the ginger, mushrooms, salt, and pepper, and bring to a boil.

4 / Mix arrowroot powder and remaining 1 cup of stock until smooth.

5 / Add powder and water mixture into soup, and lightly boil over medium-high heat for 2-4 minutes until soup starts to thicken.

6 / Beat eggs together and pour intermittently into soup.

7 / The eggs will cook very quickly (less than a minute) and then the soup is ready to go!

CREAM OF BROCCOLI
WITH TOASTED ALMONDS
FOR RITA BARDIN

Mom's mom, Nan, was a true beauty. She passed away when I was only four years old, but I love looking at her old pictures, and dreaming of what it would be like to have known her better. Luckily, I have held onto one special memory with her. When I lived in New Jersey as a little girl, Nan would take me to a local mall to go shopping. Each time, we would stop at Au Bon Pain for lunch and I would order the fluffiest almond croissant I could find. Warm and steaming, I'd crack it open and let the sweet, savory fumes engulf me. Even when Nan got very sick, she still took me shopping for our weekly outing. I keep Nan alive by asking Mom, Aunt Lauri, and Aunt Randi for stories about her. It is obvious that Nan's funny traditions and quirks have been passed down to her three girls, and now to all the grandkids. Evidently, I did not get my culinary prowess from her because her daughters fondly recall that Nan was the world's worst cook. Her definition of cooking soup was opening a can of Campbell's, and she never used herbs or spices. Her three specialties, though, were her lasagna, ribs, and a mean fried lox. Since I didn't think a fried lox soup would be all too appetizing, I instead chose this dish topped with sliced almonds, reminiscent of our Au Bon Pain adventures, placing it in a salmon colored bowl for good measure.

INGREDIENTS:

INSTRUCTIONS:

Serves: 4

Prep time:
15 minutes

Cook time:
25 minutes

1 Tbsp. coconut oil

1 medium onion, chopped

1 leek (whites and greens), sliced

1 Tbsp. garlic, chopped

½ tsp. salt

½ tsp. pepper

1 head broccoli, chopped

4 cups vegetable stock

2 cups packed fresh spinach
(about 5 oz.)

1 avocado, chopped

¼ cup sliced almonds (optional)

1 / Heat oil over medium heat.

2 / Add onion, leek, garlic, salt, and pepper, and cook for 10 minutes or until soft.

3 / Add broccoli and stock, and bring to a boil.

4 / Cover and cook for 5 minutes, until broccoli is soft.

5 / Reduce heat to low, add spinach, and cook another 2 minutes until spinach is wilted.

6 / Remove soup from heat, add avocado, and purée until smooth.

7 / Lay almonds on a foil-lined pan and toast for 4-5 minutes, turning once, watching closely so they do not burn.

8 / Serve hot, creamy soup topped with toasted almonds.

FATHER DAUGHTER BOUILLABAISSE
FOR RICHARD RAKOWSKI

If you have seen the movie *Big Fish*, you'll understand something very special about my dad; he lives his life as if in a laboratory, experimenting with people, businesses, and experiences, accumulating stories all along the way. His storytelling capabilities are truly unmatched, and most of his stories you can't possibly believe to be true. There are chance meetings with world leaders; travels across the world to meet with a Buddhist monk; and business experiments with everything from health care, to renewable energy, to soup! The beauty of it all, just like in the movie, is that the stories are all impossibly true. The experiences are real, and the effects are unparalleled. My dad has instilled his teachings in me from a very young age, and he single-handedly helped me believe in the power I have in this universe. When I was nervous entering the Miss Pre-Teen Connecticut pageant, Dad asked me if I wanted to win; I said yes, so he told me to go win – hours later I was crowned. When Dad and Melissa were ready to have children, he asked for my blessing and I gave it with one stipulation – no more daughters. They then went on to have twin boys. I told Dad about my dream to write a cookbook, and share my message and vision with the world, and he told me to follow my heart, the rest will come. Here I am now, with a published cookbook, my dad's love and support forever imprinted on my heart. We brainstormed and collaborated for countless hours over organic French coffees and smoked salmon omelets. We ate and chat, and chat and ate, and the rest is history.

For my dad's soup, there was no other choice but his famous bouillabaisse. Every time he makes it, The Drifters serenade us in the background as he tosses every type of seafood imaginable into a bubbling pot of tomatoes, onions, leeks, celery, and saffron. The process is always effortless and fun, the end product eclectic, unique, and filling, just like Dad and his love. This soup, like life, should always be an experiment. You'll never know what you'll get until you try.

INGREDIENTS:

Serves: 6-10

Prep time:
10 minutes

Cook time:
45+ minutes

2 Tbsp. olive oil

2 stalks celery, chopped

5 cloves garlic, chopped

1 onion, chopped

1 leek (whites and greens), chopped

1 cup medium/dry white wine

1 bay leaf

2 sprigs saffron

Grated zest of ½ orange

(1) 28 oz. can peeled tomatoes

¼ cup parsley, chopped

4-5 lb. mixed seafood (mussels, shrimp, white fish, lobster tails, etc.)

8+ cups water

Salt & pepper to taste

INSTRUCTIONS:

1 / Heat oil and sauté celery, garlic, onion, and leek.

2 / Add wine, bay leaf, saffron, orange zest, tomatoes, and parsley, and cook another 2-3 minutes, stirring frequently.

3 / Add seafood and enough water to cover.

4 / Cook over medium-high heat for at least 30 minutes – time on the stove is a friend to this delightful dish!

5 / Season with salt and pepper to taste, and then serve (extra napkins are recommended!).

OOP OOP SPINACH SOUP
FOR LORRIE WEXLER

Lorrie's kitchen was my home away from home growing up. When her family moved from the street over to three doors down, I loved running through the backyards, letting myself in through her back door, and plopping on an island stool to chat. If anyone can talk more than me, it is Lorrie. She would always shower me with stories, love, and a lot of food. She was training to be the best yenta and Jewish mother on the East Coast, and wouldn't let five minutes go by without offering me a "nice" sandwich, homemade cookies (using every ingredient in the pantry), or a bowl of soup — even after I dropped my bracelet into the pot she let me serve one Rosh Hashanah! Lorrie nicknamed me "Ali Oop" when I was young and has called me "Miss Oop Oop" for as long as I can remember. If I was really on her good side, I would even get an extra "Oop". Lorrie's energy in her home and in the kitchen reminds me of my own grandma — always exploding with love and joy, every ounce of food she prepared a gift. Lorrie even made a batch of homemade chicken soup for her dog, Milo, every week. Milo deserved the good stuff just like the rest of us. Over the years, Lorrie taught me so much about how to love, be myself, and find the sweetness in life. Her bowl is simple and white, leaving all of the color and exuberance to the soup itself, and the peacock feathers beneath it, speaking to Lorrie's own dynamic, quirky, and bold personality.

INGREDIENTS:

Serves: 3-4

Prep time:
10 minutes

Cook time:
45 minutes

16 cloves garlic, unpeeled

2 Tbsp. olive oil, divided

Salt & pepper

1 medium onion, chopped

16 oz. fresh spinach leaves

2+ cups chicken stock

Salt & freshly ground black pepper to taste

INSTRUCTIONS:

1 / Preheat the oven to 375 degrees.

2 / Toss the unpeeled garlic cloves with 1 Tbsp. of the oil, and a sprinkle of salt and pepper.

3 / Cover the dish with foil and bake for about 30 minutes, until browned and soft.

4 / When cooled, squeeze garlic cloves out of the peels and set aside.

5 / Heat the rest of the oil over medium heat.

6 / Add onion and sauté for 10 minutes.

7 / Add spinach and garlic, and cook for another 2 minutes.

8 / Add 2 cups of stock and purée until smooth. Add additional stock as needed until the desired consistency is reached.

9 / Season with salt and pepper to taste.

10 / Top with a drizzle of olive oil.

SUMMER

MUGS OF MELON & MINT
FOR MALLORY MARTINO

My best friend, my other half, my wifey. Mal and I met back in 2009, and from then on we've been inseparable. Our culinary adventures and memories are endless, but it all started on our first dinner date when Mal offered to make a Greek salad. I promptly told her that I hated olives, tomatoes, and feta cheese, and I saw no point in eating the cucumbers since they were over 90% water. From that moment on, Mal lovingly passed the menu planning torch to me, and the rest is history. Our favorite day ever was a warm summer day that started with a long bike ride around Lake Waramug, followed by a stop at Panini Café in Kent, CT, on the way home. We both ordered delicious sandwiches, fresh chips, and an Oreo gelato milkshake for good measure. It was one of the best meals we had ever eaten together. We sat for a long time, laughed, ate, and just enjoyed each other. To top it all off, a couple was making Mexican street corn in the middle of the Kent square and we couldn't say no! There was no talking as we shared the corn for dessert, smothered with cotija cheese, chili powder, garlic, cilantro and lime. This day in Kent sums up everything we love about our relationship – each other, sunshine-filled activities, and unforgettable shared meals.

It is seemingly impossible for life to exist for either of us without mention of the other. Mal challenges me to go after my dreams and pushes me to succeed, while loving me for me the whole way through. While I am still not a fan of Greek salad, my palate has matured as our friendship has grown. That said, I decided to design the simplest summer soup for Mal to highlight the purity of our friendship and the brightness that she has brought into my life. I am counting down the days until she moves back to Stamford to once again be my neighbor, this time sitting on the terrace, soup mugs in hand, planning our upcoming weddings together!

INGREDIENTS:

INSTRUCTIONS:

Serves: 3-4

Prep time:
10 minutes

Chill time:
2+ hours

Tip:
You can also serve this perfect summer soup in chilled martini glasses topped with melon balls wrapped in prosciutto. Enjoy!

1 cantaloupe melon, skinned & chopped

1 cup orange juice, freshly squeezed

1 Tbsp. lime juice

1 Tbsp. fresh mint, chopped (plus more to garnish)

½ cup sweet white wine (optional)

Dash of salt

1 / **Add melon, orange juice, lime juice, mint, and wine (if desired) in a food processor or blender.**

2 / **Purée until smooth.**

3 / **Add a dash of salt to taste.**

4 / **Refrigerate for at least 2 hours.**

5 / **Serve chilled topped with fresh mint.**

VERMONT PEPPER & TOMATO PURÉE
FOR HEATHER ADORISO

Without even knowing it, Heather and I lived directly next to each other when we began our post-college lives in Stamford. We were coincidentally introduced through a mutual friend and realized we were neighbors. The first time Heather invited me over for dinner, I walked next door (didn't even have to put shoes on!) and we ate a delicious meal that included fresh English peas from Stew Leonard's; as soon as I saw them out on Heather's patio, I knew our friendship was meant to be. We continued our neighborly status when I lived in Boston; Heather and her husband, Kenny, were living in the South End and I moved in just down the street. According to Ryan, it is thanks to Heather and Kenny that we are together. He said that he knew our relationship was more than a friendship after Heather and Kenny's annual "Friendsgiving" party. Her friends spent the whole night telling us how perfect we were for each other, and eventually we couldn't deny it! The four of us have had great home-cooked meals in Massachusetts, Connecticut, and even Vermont, where Heather and Kenny are from. We share a deep love for all things local and fresh, and their bowl is reminiscent of all of the cows on the beautiful farms in Vermont. For Heather, I recreated what we know as "Goodbye Soup," which we all helped create as a part of Ryan's final feast before his 15-month assignment in Dubai.

INGREDIENTS:

Serves: 4-6

Prep time:
15 minutes

Cook time:
55 minutes

2 Tbsp. olive oil

2 onions, chopped

5-10 cloves garlic, chopped

8 large bell peppers, chopped

½ tsp. salt

¼ tsp. pepper

(1) 28 oz. can organic roasted tomatoes

¼ cup basil, chopped

4 cups chicken stock

1 avocado, chopped (optional)

INSTRUCTIONS:

1 / Heat oil over medium heat.

2 / Add onions and garlic, and cook for 10 minutes until soft.

3 / Add bell peppers, salt, and pepper, stirring every few minutes for about 10 minutes until peppers begin to soften.

4 / Add roasted tomatoes, basil, and stock.

5 / Bring pot to boil and then simmer covered over medium-low heat for 35-40 minutes until peppers are soft.

6 / Let cool slightly and then purée the soup until smooth.

7 / Top with chopped avocado and a drizzle of olive oil.

COOKIE'S COCK-A-LEEKIE
FOR COOKIE WEINSTEIN

Cookie is my mom's best friend in Florida and my adopted Jewish grandma. I like to hug Cookie for a solid five minutes every time I see her to soak up all of her joy and love (she remembers our first hug, saying, "You gave me the best hug of my entire long life. No one hugs the way you do."). She is constantly exploding with smiles, laughs, and funny stories, pulling out her Yiddish at a moment's notice when she's feeling verklempt (choked up with emotion). While her name might make you think otherwise, Cookie doesn't really cook; I've asked her for homemade cookies like my grandma used to make, and she assured me I would be better off without them! While we don't share a love of baking, I do take after Cookie's ability to eat ice cream three times a day; she loves talking about it almost as much as she enjoys eating it, just like me. Her overindulgence in life simply speaks to the joy she cannot contain within. I am forever grateful for the role she plays in my life, and for all of the years of friendship and love she has shared with my mom. I know Cookie will get a kick out of the soup I chose for her from the name alone.

INGREDIENTS:

INSTRUCTIONS:

Serves: 4-6

Prep time:
15 minutes

Cook time:
90 minutes

2 Tbsp. coconut oil

6 medium leeks (whites and greens), sliced

3 carrots, peeled & chopped

2 stalks celery, chopped

3 cloves garlic, chopped

2 lb. skinless bone-in chicken thighs

4 cups chicken stock

2 cups water

1 bay leaf

½ cup flat-leaf parsley, finely chopped

12 prunes, quartered

½ tsp. salt

¼ tsp. pepper

Salt & pepper to taste

1 / Heat oil over medium-high heat.

2 / Add leeks, carrots, celery, and garlic to pot.

3 / Cook for 10 minutes over medium-high heat until lightly browned.

4 / Add chicken, stock, water, bay leaf, parsley, prunes, salt, and pepper.

5 / Boil and then simmer covered over medium-low heat for 1-1 ½ hours until chicken is falling off the bone.

6 / Remove chicken, discard bones, and shred the meat.

7 / Add the chicken back to the pot, and season with additional salt and pepper to taste.

SUMMER WATERMELON GAZPACHO
FOR NADINE DERST

My beautiful friend Dina came into my life in the summer of 2008, when she was hired as an au pair for a family in Stamford. We were dating best friends at the time who constantly wanted us to watch their soccer games, so we had a lot of opportunities to get to know each other. We "watched" game after game for hours most nights and weekends, chatting about a spectrum of topics, including the most outrageous sections from the book, *Wetlands*, she introduced me to. I in turn introduced her to her first avocado, which has since become one of her favorite foods. After Dina decided to try out being a vegetarian, I told her that I just made the most delicious turkey burger and she HAD to try it! After a few minutes of negotiating, she had a bite, loved it, and said it would be perfect with mustard. It was that moment when Dina learned about my absurd long-time fear and loathing of the condiment. When Dina had to return to Germany, we promised to stay in touch regardless of how much time passed between letters and visits. I have watched her from afar become the most caring wife and mother, and I am honored to have a beautiful bowl from her own German kitchen as a part of my project. In the spirit of our first summer together, I decided to fill Dina's bowl with a perfect soup for the hottest and sweetest season.

INGREDIENTS:

INSTRUCTIONS:

Serves: 4

Prep time:
15 minutes

Chill time:
2+ hours

4 cups watermelon, cubed & divided

1 lb. tomatoes, chopped

1 cucumber, peeled, seeded, diced, & divided

2 Tbsp. olive oil

1 Tbsp. sherry vinegar

2 Tbsp. fresh mint, chopped & divided

¾ tsp. salt, divided

¼ tsp. pepper

½ red bell pepper, diced

1 / In a blender or food processor, blend 2 ½ cups of the watermelon with all of the tomatoes and half of the cucumber.

2 / Add oil, vinegar, 1 Tbsp. of the mint, ½ tsp. of the salt, and pepper. Blend until smooth.

3 / In a separate bowl, combine remaining watermelon, cucumber, mint, and salt with bell pepper.

4 / Pour blended liquid into the bowl and stir to combine.

5 / Chill soup for at least 2 hours and then serve in chilled bowls (or martini glasses!) topped with any remaining ingredients.

ELEPHANT ORANGE, CARROT, & GINGER
FOR KELLY CARAVELLA

Kelly is my future sister-in-law, and I couldn't be luckier. Coincidentally, she is already technically my "sister" for life since we are both proud Pi Beta Phis. She is getting her PhD in Psychology, and holds all of the answers about healthy pregnancies and raising children thanks to her research. I don't see her as much as I'd like, but I always love getting the chance to be together. My favorite memories include sitting around the fire in Vermont in our PJs chatting; in return for the bubbling raspberry baked brie I made her, she would braid, unbraid, and braid my hair again. Her relationship with her brother is one that I respect and admire more than either of them will ever know. Their friendship, love, and support are impressively strong, and I can only hope to carry on those values into my own family one day.

I created this vegetarian soup for Kelly and then coincidentally found out that her favorite soup is Carrot Ginger. The ginger is great brain food to help with Kelly's studies, and the elephants who hold the soup are known to have the best memory! Kelly's grandmother loved elephants, so the mugs along with her two beautiful spoons are in honor and memory of Grammy.

INGREDIENTS:

INSTRUCTIONS:

Serves: 4-6

Prep time:
15 minutes

Cook time:
90 minutes

1 Tbsp. coconut oil

1 lb. carrots, peeled & sliced

1 sweet onion, chopped

4 cloves garlic, chopped

2 Tbsp. ginger, peeled & chopped

1 large orange, juice & zest

4 cups vegetable stock or water

1 bay leaf

Salt & pepper to taste

Pinch of nutmeg, turmeric, or ground ginger (optional)

1 / Heat oil over medium-high heat.

2 / Add carrots, onion, garlic, ginger, and 1+ Tbsp. of orange zest.

3 / Cook 10 minutes until fragrant.

4 / Add juice from the orange, stock, and bay leaf, and bring to a boil.

5 / Cover and simmer over medium-low heat for 20 minutes until carrots are soft.

6 / Purée until smooth, and season with salt and pepper to taste.

7 / Serve topped with a pinch of nutmeg, turmeric, or ginger.

PEACH LAKE ZUCCHINI & OREGANO
FOR KEVIN O'BRIEN

A vegetarian that eats bacon? Look no further. An athlete that can complete an Olympic triathlon with limited training? You got it. A man that will drive you anywhere you need to go and make sure your seat warmer is on in advance? It is possible! Kevin is a wonderful friend and we have shared many delicious meals together over the years, though his habit of having peanut M&Ms on his desk at work sticks out to me most (until the office was infested with mice as a result and his afternoon snack had to vacate the premises!). Our countless drives to work together swapping stories and sharing memories have a special place in my heart, as does his dedication to being a "big brother" for my friends and I, cheering us on when we participated in a women-only triathlon. We don't work together or live too close by anymore, but I will always appreciate the friendship and support we've shared.

For Kevin, I've created a perfect vegetarian soup to feature in his New York City-based bowl. Since he grows his own zucchini, squash, and herbs at his house on Peach Lake, there could be no other choice.

INGREDIENTS:

INSTRUCTIONS:

Serves: 4

Prep time:
5 minutes

Cook time:
20 minutes

1 lb. zucchini (3-4 cups), chopped

1 lb. leeks (whites and greens), sliced (4-5 cups)

4 cups vegetable stock or water

¼ cup fresh oregano, chopped

1 tsp. salt

Avocado oil (optional)

1 / Add all ingredients other than the avocado oil to a soup pot and bring to a boil.

2 / Simmer covered over medium-low heat for 10-15 minutes until zucchini is soft.

3 / Let soup cool slightly and then purée until smooth.

4 / Serve with a drizzle of avocado oil, a garnish of zucchini noodles, and fresh oregano.

JZ CARAMELIZED VIDALIA ONION SOUP
^{FOR} JAIME ZIMMERMAN

My favorite memory with my oldest cousin, Jonathan (JZ), and his wife, Jaime, was back when I was a high school junior on the hunt to find the perfect college. I had dreams of going to the West Coast, but my mom had visions of me staying local (within driving distance, that is). She knew I was very close-minded about her plan, so she strategically asked my cousins to take me on a college tour throughout Boston, hitting all of the major campuses from BC and BU, to Tufts and Harvard. We visited all of the schools and debriefed at the end of the night over warm, gooey chocolate chip cookies from the Doubletree Hotel. We walked all over town, and I was sneakily persuaded by the JZs to apply to Boston schools over a J.P. Licks ice cream, while Jaime conveniently pointed out all of the good-looking guys that walked by. I never ended up in Boston for college, but I always cherished that weekend we had together. When I moved there in my mid-20s, I appreciated my initial tour more than ever, and then had to suck up a big fat "I-told-you-so" from my mom.

I crafted this scrumptious summer soup for Jaime, knowing how delicious it would look in her D.C.-based red, white, and blue bowl.

INGREDIENTS:

INSTRUCTIONS:

Serves: 4

Prep time:
15 minutes

Cook time:
45 minutes

2 Tbsp. olive oil

4 medium Vidalia onions,
thinly sliced

4 cloves garlic, minced

4 cups water

1 sprig thyme (plus more to garnish)

1 bay leaf

2 tsp. salt

½ tsp. pepper

1-2 tsp. sherry vinegar

1 / Heat oil over medium heat.

2 / Add onions and garlic, and cook until caramelized, about 25 minutes (do not let the onions burn). Tip: If the onions start to brown, add a spoonful of water into the pan to loosen everything up.

3 / Reserve a cup of the onions to use as soup toppers.

4 / Add water, herbs, and spices to the remaining onions in the pan.

5 / Bring to a boil, then cover, and simmer over medium-low heat for about 15 minutes until onions are soft.

6 / Remove the thyme and bay leaf, and then purée the soup.

7 / Add the sherry vinegar to taste, and stir until well combined.

8 / Serve topped with caramelized onions and a sprig of thyme.

ROSY ROASTED TOMATO WITH FRESH BASIL PESTO
FOR RON ROZIER

I first met Ron in January of 1994, opening the door in my princess pajamas to find the man who was about to take my mom out on a blind date. "Oh, great! You brought me a big sandwich!" I exclaimed, seeing the long white box he cradled in his arms. I was crushed to find out that they were actually long-stemmed roses for Mom instead of a tasty treat for me. On date number two, I eagerly answered the door again and saw Ron with another long box. Proudly, Ron told me, "These are chocolate roses just for you," as he watched me eyeing the package. Blunt as could be, I admitted that I hated chocolate. Instead of letting my honesty get him down, Ron spent the next two decades changing my mind about this particular sweet as he has become an integral part of our family, ultimately marrying my mom! Together we've enjoyed hot dogs and beans as his first "home cooked" meal at our house (a step-up from his habit of eating one canned vegetable and a pint of Ben & Jerry's Cherry Garcia every night). Knowing how important the family meal was to my mom, Ron arrived at precisely 6:00 pm every single night so we could all eat together. He patiently and politely would eat his dinner like an angel, while the rest of us were involved in numerous antics. For a cozy, quiet meal, Ron has always loved a bowl of tomato soup with a grilled cheese. It's because of our mutual love of this meal that it was a no-brainer as to which soup I'd cook for Ron.

INGREDIENTS:

Serves: 4-6

Prep time:
20 minutes

Cook time:
90 minutes

Soup:

3 lb. Roma tomatoes, halved

2 Tbsp. olive oil, divided

Fine sea salt & pepper

1 sweet onion, chopped

1 shallot, chopped

1 heaping Tbsp. garlic, chopped

½ cup packed fresh basil
(about 20 leaves)

(1) 15 oz. can tomatoes, diced
(organic, no salt added)

1 qt. vegetable stock

Pesto:

4 oz. fresh basil

2-3 Tbsp. olive oil

2 tsp. crushed garlic

¼ cup pine nuts

½ tsp. sea salt

¼ tsp. pepper

INSTRUCTIONS:

1 / **Preheat oven to 400 degrees.**

2 / **Slice tomatoes length-wise and arrange on a foil-lined baking sheet.**

3 / **Drizzle 1 Tbsp. of oil over tomatoes, and season with sea salt and pepper.**

4 / **Roast tomatoes for 45 minutes.**

5 / **Meanwhile, make the pesto: Pulse basil in a food processor. Add all remaining ingredients, blending until smooth. You may need to scrape down the sides so everything mixes well. Add additional pine nuts or olive oil if you prefer your pesto thicker or thinner.**

6 / **In a large soup pot, heat remaining 1 Tbsp. of oil over medium heat, and add onion, shallot, and garlic. Cook 10 minutes until tender.**

7 / **Add basil, canned tomatoes, stock, and roasted tomatoes, and bring to a boil.**

8 / **Simmer covered over medium-low heat for 30 minutes.**

9 / **Purée the soup until smooth, and serve piping hot, topped with a drizzle of fresh pesto.**

LAKE HOUSE NECTARINES WITH CRISPY PROSCIUTTO

FOR RYAN CARAVELLA

Ryan's and my love story can be told completely in food. We've trekked to farmers markets from Vermont to Colorado, and everywhere in between. We've snacked and chatted along the way on countless road trips, and our favorite memories with friends and family revolve around the dinner table. Our most romantic meal took place at the end of a gorgeous pier in the middle of the Persian Gulf in Dubai, and our most memorable meal at our favorite restaurant began with Ryan on one knee proposing to me. Ryan indulges my love for food with an open mind and heart, supporting every single recipe and endeavor I undertake; that includes this very cookbook, which has led to troughs and troughs of leftover soup that he has been more than happy to consume, despite claiming he hated soup when it all began! Of all the meals over the years, the most impactful was one that took place at Ryan's family's lake house in the summer of 2012. The stars aligned that night when our steak caught on fire, only to become the most scrumptious medium rare piece of meat either of us had ever eaten. We prepared an incredible feast together, including grilled peaches topped with fresh basil and prosciutto. We ate our food under the stars, realizing that our friendship was unmatched, our partnership effortless, and our bond undeniable. The perfect man, the perfect food, and the perfect night with the stars out overhead created just the right environment for me to realize that the one true love of my life had been right in front of me the whole time. For my fiancé's soup, I aimed to capture that evening in a bowl.

INGREDIENTS:

Serves: 4-6

Prep time:
10 minutes

Cook time:
45 minutes, plus
2+ hours to chill

6 nectarines, halved & pitted

1 Tbsp. coconut oil, divided

Pinch of fine sea salt

1 sweet onion, chopped

2 cups vegetable stock or water

½ cup orange juice, freshly squeezed (optional)

6 slices prosciutto about 3 oz. total)

1 lemon

INSTRUCTIONS:

1 / **Preheat oven to 450 degrees.**

2 / **Brush nectarines with ½ Tbsp. melted coconut oil and a pinch of fine sea salt.**

3 / **Lay nectarines face down on a baking sheet and cook for 10 minutes.**

4 / **Flip and cook another 10-15 minutes until lightly browned.**

5 / **In the meantime, heat remaining coconut oil over medium heat.**

6 / **Add onion and cook for 5-10 minutes until translucent.**

7 / **Add nectarines and stock or water.**

8 / **Bring to a boil and then lower to a simmer for 10 minutes.**

9 / **Purée until smooth.**

10 / **Add orange juice if desired and chill for at least 2 hours.**

11 / **Just prior to serving, preheat oven to 400 degrees.**

12 / **Lay prosciutto on a foil- or parchment-lined baking sheet, and bake 10-15 minutes, flipping once until meat darkens and fat lightly browns.**

13 / **Lay prosciutto on a plate with paper towels – it will continue to crisp up as it cools.**

14 / **Serve chilled soup topped with crisp prosciutto and a squeeze of fresh lemon.**

SKINNI NANNI SUMMER SQUASH PURÉE
FOR LAURI ZIMMERMAN

My mom's older sister happens to be my favorite and most successful health coaching client. Aunt Lauri underwent a complete emotional, mental, and physical transformation when we began to work together on her diet and lifestyle. I couldn't be happier for her, especially after everything she's done for me over the years. Aunt Lauri lives only 20 minutes away, and has always been an incredible stand-in mom when my own was too far for a visit. She taught me how to take deep breaths when life gets to be a little too much, and when to get manicures (weekly, when you have a boyfriend who's about to propose...). I have watched her transform over the years into the most well-loved nanni of seven beautiful grandchildren and, through it all, she has always found the time to treat me like a daughter of her own. Aunt Lauri deserved a pure soup considering it's now been over a year since she completely overhauled her diet, appreciating the simplest of ingredients and flavors. Coupled with her beautiful bowl, this dish perfectly combines her celebrated simplicity with a renewed sense of vibrancy.

INGREDIENTS:

INSTRUCTIONS:

Serves: 4

Prep time:
3 hours to soak cashews + 10 minutes

Cook time:
30 minutes

2-2½ lb. summer squash, seeded & sliced

1 medium sweet onion, sliced

2 large leeks (whites only), sliced

3 cloves garlic, sliced

2 Tbsp. olive oil

Dash of salt & pepper

1 cup raw cashews, soaked for at least 3 hours & drained

3-4 cups filtered water

Salt & pepper to taste

2 Tbsp. lemon juice (optional)

Basil leaves (optional)

Yellow cherry tomatoes (to garnish)

Cracked black pepper (to garnish)

1 / Preheat oven to **425 degrees.**

2 / Arrange summer squash, onion, leeks, and garlic on a foil- or parchment-lined baking pan.

3 / Drizzle oil over veggies, sprinkle with a dash of salt and pepper, and mix to combine.

4 / Roast for **25 minutes** until lightly browned.

5 / Transfer veggies to a food processor or blender, and add the cashews and water.

6 / Purée soup until well combined, and then season with salt and pepper to taste.
Tip: You can add lemon juice and basil into the purée to kick the taste up a notch.

7 / Top with yellow cherry tomatoes and some cracked black pepper.

TRIED & TRUE GAZPACHO
FOR PAM & RICK MARTINO

There are a few things I know that I can always count on with the Martinos: Mrs. M will bring me themed socks and delicious-smelling hand soap for every season and major holiday; and Mr. M will rave about the Red Sox while grilling perfectly seasoned chicken, his Bose sound system playing in the background. Most importantly, they will always remind me that I am their third daughter, and a true part of the family. One Christmas Eve, Mr. M even went to great lengths to cook a Paleo version of his famous lasagna, handing me the platter with pride when he took it from the oven, his desire to make me feel welcome, comfortable, and loved written all over his face. Truly my chosen family, Mr. and Mrs. M are the best adopted parents a girl could ask for; they raised my most special friend in the world, and they have instilled their incredible values of generosity, loyalty, and love in me as well.

This particular soup was chosen for them because Mrs. M always makes the best gazpacho. Her tried and true recipe, on a tattered paper barely legible from college, is now adapted for *Bowls of Love*, and printed safely for the years to come.

INGREDIENTS:

Serves: 4

Prep time:
20 minutes

Chill time:
2+ hours

3 large tomatoes, chopped

½ jalapeño, diced (or more if you like it super spicy!)

2 cloves garlic, diced

Juice from 1 lemon

Juice from 1 lime

¼ cup olive oil

2 Tbsp. balsamic vinegar

½ medium red onion, diced

1 cucumber, peeled, seeded, & diced

1 green bell pepper, diced

¼ cup basil, chopped

½ cup cilantro, chopped

1½ tsp. fine sea salt

½ tsp. pepper

INSTRUCTIONS:

1 / Add tomatoes, jalapeño, garlic, lemon juice, lime juice, olive oil, and balsamic vinegar to a food processor or blender, and blend until well combined.

2 / In a bowl, combine onion, cucumber, bell pepper, basil, cilantro, salt, and pepper.

3 / Add half of the bowl to the blender and blend until mixed.

4 / Pour liquid gazpacho over remaining ingredients in the bowl.

5 / Chill for at least 2 hours (preferably overnight).

6 / Serve cold, topped with extra ingredients.

RED HAWK RANCH CHILLED AVOCADO & CUCUMBER SOUP
FOR TIM SILVERA

Tim was a financial services client of mine back when I was a consultant. He soon became my favorite client when a surprise delivery of beautiful avocados arrived at my desk at work. It turned out that Tim's family founded a ranch back in 1971. It started as a small parcel sequestered upon the side of a hill, and it was there, looking out at the blue California sky and the rim of a beautiful mountain range, smelling the faint brine of the ocean and listening to the wind rustle the trees, that Tim decided it was the perfect sort of place to start up a family run business. He was right. Tim's family watched their avocado trees closely, observing them grow until they were beautifully ripe with rich and buttery flesh. They decided that the discovery of such a beautiful harvest should be shared with the world. You can now go to their website at **rhravocados.com** and order freshly picked avocados from Red Hawk Ranch, delivered straight to your door. You can try it out for a guacamole party on Cinco de Mayo or when you're looking for a cool, refreshing soup like the one I made for Tim.

INGREDIENTS:

INSTRUCTIONS:

Serves: 4-6

Prep time:
15 minutes

Chill time:
30+ minutes

Tip:
The ataulfo mangoes are also known as baby, yellow, honey, or champagne mangoes. They are smaller and often sweeter than the traditional "Tommy Atkins" mango sold in the U.S.

Soup:
2 English cucumbers, peeled, seeded, & chopped

2 avocados, chopped

1 tsp. lime zest

⅓ cup cilantro (plus more to garnish)

2 scallions, chopped

1 tsp. fine sea salt

½ tsp. pepper

2 Tbsp. fresh lime juice

Salsa:
1 ataulfo mango, diced

½ red bell pepper, diced

1 large tomato, diced

1 Tbsp. fresh cilantro, chopped

1 tsp. lime juice

Dash of salt, pepper, & garlic powder

1 tsp. olive oil (optional)

1 / **Purée all soup ingredients in a blender or food processor.**

2 / **Refrigerate for at least 30 minutes.**

3 / **Meanwhile, add all ingredients for the salsa in a bowl, and refrigerate until the soup is fully chilled.**

4 / **Once chilled, serve the soup with a dollop of mango salsa.**

WHO'S TO THANK?

This book was a team effort in every sense. I am eternally grateful to the crew of lovely ladies that helped turn my dream into a reality:

ERICA: for capturing the beauty in every dish I created. A picture is worth 1,000 words and, while I'll never stop talking, your photos tell the whole story.

MARGOT: for conveying my message with such creative and intuitive design. You brought my brand and ideas to life, and I couldn't have asked for a better designer.

A.J.: for convincing me that my blog could be a book and I was worthy of being a published author. Your encouragement and support exceeded all expectations. You listened to me on the phone for countless hours and helped turn my ramblings into words. I am your biggest fan and a friend for life.

To the 199 people who contributed to my Kickstarter campaign and helped fund this project – you are the original soldiers backing the message of *Bowls of Love*, and I can assure you that you will be rewarded with good karma. An extra special thanks to my soup-er, soup-erior, and soup-reme supporters:

Soup-er Supporters

Alan E. London
Andrew Stern
Angelo Brancadoro
Angie Doan
Ann Goodson & Kevin Daley
Aroldo de Rienzo
Carl Larouche
Carolyn Malloy
Devung Mahajan
Evan & Catherine Rakowski
Gillian Pressman
Hilary Pearl
Howard Teich
James Ditter

Joann Braun
Jon Leatherbury
Judy & Lou Caravella
Justin Kuchta
Kara Salvagno
Katie Malone
Kevin O'Brien
Kevin Raynes
Lauri & Bill Zimmerman
Leon Hanna
Liz Lanza
Mallory Martino
Margot George
Marla Garchik

Melinda Martino
Melissa Sproch
Nadine Derst
Pruitt Chamness
Rachel Fitzmaurice
Rami Karjian
Randi & Gary Topche
Richard Rakowski
Ricky Chu
Rob Northway
Ryan Caravella
Sarah Bowling
Steph Salvagno
Steve Shaer

Soup-erior Supporters

Bridgett Luther
David Caravella
Jean Christophe Pietri
Karl James & Co (Karl Robe)

Laura Daley
Linda Hartz
Pam & Rick Martino
Tim Silvera

Soup-reme Supporters

Vikki & Ron Rozier

INDEX

* Ingredients are listed as vegetables although, botanically speaking, they are technically fruits. They are organized in this way to help support an organized shopping experience and align with conventional thought.

**These ingredients are soup staples and are included in the majority of the recipes in this book.

NOTES